KT-525-328

SUPPORTING
EVERY CHILD

Second Edition

Editors
**Anita Walton
and Gillian Goddard**

Los Angeles | London | New Delhi
Singapore | Washington DC

www.learningmatters.co.uk

Los Angeles | London | New Delhi
Singapore | Washington DC

www.learningmatters.co.uk

Learning Matters
An imprint of SAGE Publications Ltd
1 Oliver's Yard
55 City Road
London EC1Y 1SP

SAGE Publications Inc
2455 Teller Road
Thousand Oaks, California 91320

SAGE Publications India PVT LTD
B1/I 1 Mohan Cooperative Industrial Area
Malthura Road
New Dehli 110 044

SAGE Publications Asia-Pacific Pte Ltd
3 Church Street
#10-04 Samsung Hub
Singapore 049483

© 2012 Jacqui Basquill, Karen Boardman,
Karen Castle, Linda Dunne, Sue Farragher,
Gillian Goddard, Susan Graves,
Maureen Judge, Alexis Moore, Felix Obadan,
Lisa O'Connor, Joanne Sutcliffe, Anita Walton

This edition published in 2012

First published in 2009

Apart from any fair dealing for the purposes of
research or private study, or criticism or
review, as permitted under the Copyright,
Design and Patents Act, 1988, this publication
may be reproduced, stored or transmitted in
any form, or by any means, only with the prior
permission in writing of the publishers, or in
the case of reprographic reproduction, in
accordance with the terms of licences issued
by the Copyright Licensing Agency. Enquiries
concerning reproduction outside these terms
should be sent to the publishers.

Library of Congress Control Number:
2012933562

British Library Cataloguing in Publication Data

A catalogue record for this book is available
from the British Library.

ISBN: 978 0 85725 821 2 paperback
ISBN: 978 0 85725 878 6 hardback

Editor: Amy Thornton
Development Editor: Jennifer Clark
Production Controller: Chris Marke
Project Management: Diana Chambers
Marketing Manager: Catherine Slinn
Cover Design: Topics
Typeset by: Kelly Winter
Printed by: TJ International Ltd, Padstow, Cornwall

MIX
Paper from
responsible sources
FSC
www.fsc.org   FSC® C013056

Contents

1 THE ROLE AND SCOPE OF SUPPORT STAFF IN EDUCATION PRACTICE

Gillian Goddard

CHAPTER OBJECTIVES

By the end of this chapter you will:

- have greater awareness of the distinctive contribution of support staff to education practice;
- be aware of the range of roles that encompass educational support;
- be able to reflect on professional boundaries in roles;
- recognise the challenges and opportunities facing support staff in today's educational settings.

LINKS TO **HLTA** STANDARDS

1. To communicate effectively and sensitively with children, young people, colleagues, parents and carers.

2. To demonstrate the commitment to collaborative and cooperative working with colleagues.

3. To improve their own knowledge and practice.

Introduction

When I was a child in the sixties I was taught by teachers, one per classroom. The only other adults in school were lunchtime welfare assistants, or dinner ladies as we called them (a very few – there were always teachers on duty) and the caretaker and school secretary. Of course, there were cleaners but I didn't see them. In reception class there was probably a nursery nurse but I have no memory of one. In secondary school there was an odd science technician in a white coat who hid in small rooms packed with equipment. Now in schools there is a whole range of paraprofessionals who form part of the educational team: many of these are in educational 'support' roles. This chapter will discuss the essential nature of the support role as distinct from that of the teacher and identify the range of roles occurring in schools and other education settings today. It will also consider the challenges that can face support staff, especially in relation to role boundaries, and the opportunities for role development.

Why the expansion of educational support staff?

There will be greater discussion of the history of the development of professional roles of support staff in Chapter 2, but for this chapter you will need to know that there were four major drivers that led to the expansion of support staff in schools over the past two decades. As early as 1967 the Plowden Report on Primary Education identified the value of support staff assisting in the teaching of children (Plowden, 1967). However, it was only with the advent of an inclusive education agenda (DfEE, 1997), which sought to educate as many children with special educational needs (SEN) as possible within mainstream settings, that the numbers of classroom support staff expanded. This brought about the widespread use of 'Special Support Assistants' (such as Teaching Assistants) to work with individual 'statemented' children within class, to enable them to access learning (DfES, 2001). In secondary schools, the principal support role is the Special Support Assistant.

The second driver that led to the expansion of support roles in primary settings was the pressure to raise standards in numeracy and literacy achievement. This began in earnest with the imposition of the National Strategies for Literacy and Numeracy in 1998/9 (DfEE, 1998, 1999). The outcome was a very complex pattern of teaching in the primary classroom that relied on group work of differentiated and/or varied tasks, needing supervision and support by more than one adult. As a consequence, classroom assistants were employed to supervise and work with small groups, most commonly the 'lower ability' groups, to ensure that the lesson outcomes were achieved. They were often only employed during morning school when these core subjects tended to be taught.

Later, in the first decade of the twenty-first century, initiatives to 'boost' Standard Assessment Tests (SATs) achievement in the core subjects led to the deployment of skilled and advanced Teaching Assistants (those who, for example, had obtained Level 3 NVQ qualifications), to deliver intervention programmes with those pupils identified as benefitting from short-term targeted withdrawal work in numeracy and literacy. This use of support staff for intervention work spread to secondary schools as the pressure to raise the level of achievement in SATs and GCSEs was increased.

The new demands on teachers led to discontent and many teachers left the profession. This became such a concern for Government that it undertook a review of teaching roles and, in conjunction with unions, it agreed to workforce reforms that guaranteed teaching staff planning and preparation time for lessons as part of the working week (ATL/DfES, 2003). As part of these reforms the use of support staff in the classroom to take over routine tasks and to offer operational assistance to the teacher (be their right-hand woman/man) was promoted. In primary settings it became the norm for each class to have its own Teaching Assistant (TA).

Finally, the widening of education to include the education of the whole child became Government policy through its implementation of the *Every Child Matters (ECM) Agenda* (DfES, 2003). This, together with the advent of the widening of universal education to include three- and four-year olds, resulted in the development of more paraprofessional support roles linked to attendance, parental outreach, pastoral support and the management of children who were at risk of exclusion.

Learning mentors, inclusion officers, behaviour and attendance officers, and outreach workers all began to appear in the mid 2000s. In the new Children's Centres and Sure Start Centres key workers were evolving to work with families with young children to support the achievement of the ECM Five Outcomes (DfES, 2003), with particular focus on safeguarding, health monitoring and promotion, early years education and the development of parenting skills.

Support role versus teaching role

REFLECTIVE TASK

Draw a spider diagram with 'the teacher's role' in the centre of it. Now identify as many specific jobs they have to do to teach.

Now repeat this exercise for the support staff role. Avoid going into specific tasks you are assigned to but think rather in terms of a general job description.

Now identify the differences between the roles of support staff and those of teachers. Although they are similar, there are differences as support staff students realise when they transfer to teacher training courses, and teachers realise when they give up teaching and take a job as a TA.

What are the differences?

The word 'support' means many things. According to a dictionary definition it can mean:

> *to carry part of weight of, hold up, keep from falling or sinking . . . to give strength to, encourage . . . tolerate, supply with necessities, lend assistance to, to back up, take a secondary part to, assist by one's presence*
>
> (Sykes, *Concise OED*, 1975, 1160–1).

This is a rather apt set of definitions as most of the support staff roles involve just such a set of roles and relationships. It is interesting that built into a support role is a positive relationship with the one being supported (the pupil in this case), but also a relationship of support with the teacher.

Similarly, a teacher is defined as one who *enables [a person] or causes by instruction and training, compels by punishment etc to do, give lessons in school . . . explain, show, state by way of instruction.* (Sykes, *Concise OED*, 1974, 1186–7)

Although support staff often find themselves teaching or tutoring pupils and using the teaching skills of planning, explaining, instructing, questioning, monitoring and assessing, these are usually under the auspices and direction of the teacher. The teacher takes responsibility for the learning of his/her class. They are expected to plan for all subjects, deliver the curriculum and make judgements about achievement. The teacher is also the named and legal person responsible for the safety, well-being and care of all the children in the class. The support staff member in class works under the authority and direction of the class teacher to assist him/her in the achievement of their role. Higher Level Teaching Assistants (HLTAs) who have demonstrated the HLTA Standards (TDA, 2006b) can teach whole classes and plan for the same; nonetheless, it has to be with the approval and under the responsibility of the teacher.

Implicit in our twin definitions is also the difference in main focus. The teacher's job is to educate predominantly; the support staff role is to help, assist and encourage. The support staff main focus centres on that of the emotional, motivational and pastoral realms. The relationship between pupil and teacher, and TA and pupil, is frequently different. The latter is more personal, more like that of a parent. The teacher's role is governed by the urgency of the purpose of teaching and is backed up by authority and judgement decisions. Support staff tend towards persuasion, encouragement and individualised responses; there is authority, but the focus is understanding and helping the whole child, not simply achieving a set of learning outcomes. Ultimately, however, both are working towards helping children learn and achieve.

> **REFLECTIVE TASK**
>
> If you are presently working or volunteering in an education setting or have some experience of the support staff roles in these settings, then reflect on the ways you were or are 'different' from a teacher in what you do and offer to pupils.

The relationship with the teacher is also different from that between two teachers. You may feel that in your experience what stands out in this relationship is hierarchy, with the support staff member having less power, less status, less knowledge and less recognition in importance and pay (Edmond and Price, 2009; Goddard et al., 2008). However, the relationship is also frequently marked with a mutual interdependence and mutual respect, where the differing roles merge together to achieve more than could be achieved without the other. This acknowledgement of the different but significant contributions support staff play in the education purpose is at the heart of contemporary and successful education practice.

Support staff roles and the issue of role boundaries

As has been discussed, there are many varied roles for support staff in schools and education settings; indeed, the creation of a specific support staff role often evolves from a combination of an individual's strengths and willingness to adapt and develop, and a specific need in a school, class or with a pupil (Edmond and Price, 2009; Tucker, 2009). Thus, many of you may be in unique roles which have been carved out for you in that setting.

The problem with evolving rather than fixed roles is that there can be occasions when the support staff member is either being asked to, or wants to, overstep their 'normal' role boundaries and do something more or something different. When this over-stepping comes from the teacher or the head teacher or special educational needs coordinator (SENCO) it can be hard to refuse. Fears of being seen as inflexible and uninterested or truculent tend to result in a TA taking on something they feel ill-suited to, or untrained in, something that takes more of their free unpaid time or something beyond their skills level which might lead to failure. When the change of role is initiated by the TA themselves, it could be trespassing on other professional boundaries, could be taking the TA into areas of incompetence that would do harm not good, or something which takes more time than the TA is being paid for. Equally, both situations could be exciting, stimulating, opportunities for growth personally and professionally, and a means of increasing their knowledge and recognition as well as leading to innovation in school practice and greater success for the school and its pupils. The following case studies will identify some of the key support roles that exist in many schools today and address some of the issues around role boundaries.

The Teaching Assistant

This support staff role usually requires working with one class or department and involves supporting the teacher/s and pupils directly in their learning, by helping with resources and administration for teachers, and by working with small groups in class time to help learning under the direction of the teacher. This group work is a major feature of primary classrooms but less so in secondary schools. The TA has grades of responsibilities with the first grade being administrative and helping the teacher but not working with children; the second involves a mixture of the two and the third grade involves some planning, teaching and assessing of some or half the class, some supervision and some additional responsibilities such as supervising the reading books home system (TDA, 2008; Ofsted 2008). Vocational Qualifications exist to match these grades. In all three situations, however, the class teacher/head of department remains the one responsible for the work of the TA.

Case Study 1: Jamie the Teaching Assistant

Jamie is a part-time level 1 Teaching Assistant in a primary school. She works in the Year 4 class under the supervision and direction of the class teacher. She photocopies, helps with displays, and helps get out and put away resources. Her main work during class time is to support groups of children with their numeracy and literacy work. She is given an activity plan by the teacher that tells her what the objective for the group is and what to do. She usually works with the children who struggle with maths and English. Jamie really enjoys this work and wants to get her NVQ Level 2 qualification so that she can achieve promotion and do more work with pupils. She enjoys helping the children understand the point of what they are doing and she tries to ensure that the activities are fun, though she is conscious that she must keep the noise down.

The children seem to relish working with her. Sometimes they talk to her about their home lives or when they are worried about something. Jamie listens sympathetically and once or twice has felt obliged to pass on the information she has been given to the teacher, having told the pupil she would need to do this. She worries a bit about a couple of pupils who seem unloved and unhappy. She brought in some of her own children's old PE kit so that, if these pupils forget their kit, she can lend it to them. She wishes she could do more but knows it wouldn't be right. It would be interfering and offensive to the parents and unfair to the other pupils in the class.

REFLECTIVE TASK
- Looking at case study 1, identify Jamie's main role and jot down a few bullet points that would form her job description if we had one.

On the surface you might assume that Jamie is actually not at risk of overstepping her role boundaries, but Jamie is being drawn towards intervening pastorally with individual children. Is Jamie right in her final thoughts? Will she act anyway and if so how? There is no right or wrong answer here, but think through the advantages of intervention and the problems that might occur if she did interfere. Would she be overstepping her boundaries and would that be a problem or an advantage to the school, pupils or her?

Special Support Assistants

Special Support Assistants (SSAs) are often contracted and employed to support a particular child or sometimes two or three children, all of whom have statements for SEN and for whom the school receives additional funding to ensure learning. The contract of employment is often temporary, term time only and usually limited in contact hours. SSAs, in addition to direct assistance to the pupil with SEN, often act as advocates for the child and also liaise closely with parents, frequently taking on the role of intermediary in communications and disputes.

CASE STUDY 2: MARTIN THE SSA

Martin is a full-time level 2 learning support assistant in an urban high school, having formally been a science technician in the same school. He spends his day supporting Sam, a Year 8 boy, with a statement for autistic spectrum disorder. He accompanies the boy to his classes and then works one-to-one with him to help him cope with the pace and variation of the lessons. He adapts resources when he's given the chance, though mostly he has to do this 'on the hoof' as teachers hand out worksheets. The boy enjoys maths and science's and behaves well in these sessions. His achievement in these areas in good, but in English he becomes frustrated and doesn't understand inferences and demands for aesthetic appreciation of the text. Although he can read, he has times when he refuses to take part and can become aggressive and withdrawn. Sometimes Martin is allowed to withdraw Sam from the English class and teach him one-to-one. The school considers this anti-inclusionary, but the English teacher finds it a relief when permission is given for Martin to withdraw Sam.

Martin accompanies Sam on his breaks, though he tries to keep in the background to avoid making Sam dependent upon him socially. What he does do is watch for signs that Sam is being taunted, made fun of or wound up deliberately by other pupils. Twice he has intervened on Sam's behalf when he was being bullied. Martin reported the incidents and the school acted to stop that behaviour. Martin considers that the other pupils tolerate Sam because he doesn't want to interfere in their groups or sports, but he also believes Sam may be lonely. He has plans to begin an after-school science club, which he thinks would bring Sam into contact with other science enthusiasts. He spends the end of his day talking to Sam's mum over the phone (Sam is taxied home), briefing her about Sam's day. Once a term, Martin gives a report to the SENCO on Sam's progress with his targets and attends the Individual Education Plan (IEP) review meeting with Sam.

REFLECTIVE TASK
- Looking at case study 2, construct the likely job description Martin was given when he started.

In what ways is Martin pushing the boundaries of his role? In what ways is what he is proposing and doing an advantage or a problem for the school/pupils/himself?

Learning Mentors

Learning Mentors were introduced as part of the then Government's 1999 Excellence in Cities initiative to help support children at risk of exclusion or who were frequent non-attenders to attend, behave and achieve better (Edmond and Price, 2009). Learning Mentors had two main roles when they were introduced: to improve behaviour and remove barriers to learning so that individual pupils could go on and achieve. Their role has developed greatly and expanded, so that most schools in deprived areas have learning mentors in place. They have a recognised pastoral role and frequently work one-to-one with pupils or withdraw small groups to work on personal and social development issues such as self-esteem or anger management. They also tend to lead in parental liaison and support.

CASE STUDY 3: KATHERINE, THE LEARNING MENTOR

Katherine is a full-time level 4 learning mentor in a primary school in an area of extreme social deprivation where there is a prevailing culture of unemployment. The school takes most of the pupils previously excluded from the other schools in the area, thus the school has a very high number of children statemented for emotional, social and behavioural difficulties. There is a low achievement rate for National Tests and a problem with attendance. Despite this, the staff is highly committed to its role in raising aspirations, and the environment is one characterised by its calmness, colourful displays and care.

Katherine's role is multifarious. She begins her day at 8.20 a.m. by calling at the homes of five pupils who struggle to attend and encouraging them to come with her to school. When she arrives with her pupils she goes into a staff briefing, which includes her valuable update on the well-being of her five reluctant pupils. While morning assembly is going on she has a meeting with 12 pupils for whom she has special responsibility. She celebrates the successes of the day before, reminds them of their learning and behaviour targets and encourages them to 'keep cool and tuned in'. She gives them the times in the day when she will be withdrawing them from class to work on the social and emotional skills in her own classroom area. Throughout the meeting the children eat as much hot toast as they want and drink orange juice. They finish with a group hug and a rallying cry of 'we're great, we can do it!'

After classes begin, she takes her groups for SEAL-inspired games and activities that conclude with a calming story and soft music (SEAL refers to Social and Emotional Aspects of Learning). During break time she goes out to the playground and watches her pupils. Frequently she is involved in helping the pupils negotiate conflict and defuse aggression. The teachers really value her for this intermediary role.

Her sessions continue in the late morning, then at lunchtime she spends the time offering a drop-in chat session. This is open to all pupils, not just those for whom she has special responsibility.

In the afternoon she is involved in supporting a pupil who has lost his temper and thrown a chair at a teacher. He's run off, but soon returns to school. She talks to him, calming him down and then going with him to the head teacher, where he is temporarily excluded. As his lone parent is not available, Katherine keeps him with her until the end of the day, when she walks him back to his home and talks to his dad about the incident.

Finally, she goes home, having made notes on the encounter. Tomorrow is another day.

REFLECTIVE TASK
Looking at case study 3:

- What statements would be on her job description?
- What benefits to the school and the pupils does she bring?
- What could be problematic for Katherine in this wide-ranging role?

Family outreach worker

Outreach workers began to appear as a direct result of the Government Sure Start Initiatives to raise the life chances of the 0–5s (NESS, 2002). They tended to work from Children's Centres or Sure Start Centres but sometimes they work in schools in particularly deprived areas or sometimes for the local authority to support travelling communities or refugee families. Their focus is on the supporting, encouraging, educating and training of parents so that their children can achieve a better life and education outcome. They act also in advocacy roles and guide parents towards other specialist support services and to new opportunities in learning and self-development. Their ultimate focus is not the parents but the children and as such they also liaise closely with GPs and social services.

CASE STUDY 4: JOHN, THE FAMILY OUTREACH WORKER

John works from a Children's Centre attached to a secondary school in a very deprived area of a city. He has a case load of fifteen families that he is currently supporting. Today he's been asked to make a preliminary visit to a family referred to him by the school. This family has two sons in secondary school and three children in primary. The two boys in secondary are showing signs of general but not severe neglect and are tired and can be aggressive and defiant. They generally respond to behaviour management strategies, but they are achieving less well each term, and seem worried and anxious quite a lot of the time. The learning mentor managed to establish that the sole carer, their mum, is not coping very well at home since their dad left and their gran died, and it falls to the lads to look out for the others and get them fed. The mother hasn't responded to any requests by the school to attend and discuss the children.

John has already put through a call to mum and spoken to her. She was willing for John to visit to see if there was any help that could be given to her, but she sounded depressed and defeated and slightly fearful of official interference. 'You're not the social services?' she had asked. When John calls at the house, the mother is at first reluctant to let him in. John is okay with that and suggests meeting at another time at the Children's Centre or even at the local shopping centre cafe. In the end he does get invited in and, using his listening skills, his compassion and non-judgemental approach with observation of her and the environment, he develops a good initial understanding of what she is trying to cope with and what she finds really hard. She begins to open up to him about her guilt in being a bad mother and her loss of her mum on whom she depended for much of her practical and psychological support. John suggests that the local free bereavement service might help her. She had said she needs to talk to someone; she can't talk to the kids about how she feels now her mum's died. He also offers the possibility of him coming regularly to help her learn some techniques for behaviour management and the setting of routines in the house, so that the children wouldn't be so challenging for her and she could feel less tired and defeated. She agrees to this but John senses that she is hoping John will just do all this for her. John stresses the benefits of her being able to use these skills to make life easier when he isn't there. He agrees to come again the following day and talk about the things that wind her up with the children and ways of managing so that she doesn't get mad or just give up.

When he gets back he writes up his notes and sets a time frame for some key objectives to be achieved. He phones the bereavement service and confirms a contact name and gauges the length of the waiting list. He writes this down for his client.

In the afternoon he runs a parent support group of dads alone, including some practical cookery.

As he is leaving, a parent he has worked with in the past calls in upset and needing to talk. He makes her coffee and sits listening to her difficulties, and then reminds her of a couple of strategies they had practised and also suggests she ask for some help from the school pastoral support team. He agrees to go with her to that meeting if she wants him to do that. She agrees and asks if he would phone the school for her. He hands her the phone but dials the number and she copes fine with that, agreeing a date and time both can do with the school learning mentor. She goes off really much more positive and feeling better. He has written the date and time down and will give her a call on the day of the meeting to remind her about it.

As he is leaving for the car park, he wonders if he should call in at his morning client's house for half an hour and see how she is with the children. It would be unannounced and he doesn't like doing that. In the end he doesn't, he goes home. He has to prepare for his supervision meeting with his boss tomorrow where he reviews his cases and he needs to make some notes on that.

REFLECTIVE TASK
- What would appear on John's job description?
- Are there any issues of role boundary here? If so, what is causing them?
- What might be problematic for John, or the service, or the families in John's work?

Higher Level Teaching Assistants

HLTAs were brought in on the back of Workforce Reforms to enable a TA to take responsibility for whole class teaching, under the direction of the teacher and also to undertake highly responsible support roles in school (TDA, 2006a). HLTAs have to demonstrate that they have met all the HLTA standards and have sufficient knowledge and skills to work alone with a class and for the children to achieve (TDA, 2006b).

CASE STUDY 5: HANNAH THE HLTA
Hannah works in a large primary school in an urban setting. The catchment area is mixed. She obtained her HLTA status five weeks ago and up till now she had been working on the delivery of intervention programmes for literacy and numeracy and she runs the After School Club. She has now been asked to cover for a teacher in one of the Y3 classes, who is going to be off sick for several weeks.

She knows some of the pupils but not all. Hannah is paid at level 3 rate (not HLTA level 4 rate) for 25 hours a week (9–3 p.m. with an hour for lunch).

She feels she should accept this challenge even though she feels it is a bit of a leap from covering a session once a week in a scheduled and planned way. She does the Y6 class-teacher's planning, preparation and assessment (PPA) time by teaching a scheme of work one afternoon a week on personal, social and health education using the SEAL materials (DfES, 2005). She is also worried about her intervention groups, which clearly will now not be staffed, or staffed by another TA. She is anxious about whether she could cope with the planning of the whole curriculum full time and the marking workload on top of running the After School Club, which she is paid for separately. The Head assures her all will be well and she will be just fine getting stuck in. The Head has every faith in her ability. He suggests she have a chat with the other Y3 teachers to get their ideas on what is to be taught this term.

REFLECTIVE TASK

- In what ways, if any, is Hannah being asked to over-step her role boundaries?
- What advice would you give to her as a concerned colleague that would help her negotiate a change of situation here?

These few roles represent only a very few of the type currently being practised in schools and education settings. I haven't mentioned the Nursery Care Assistant, or the Cover Supervisor, the Lunchtime Welfare Assistant, or the behaviour and attendance officer, or inclusion officer, or many others.

PRACTICAL TASK

- Seek out your own job description if you have one or write your own.
- See what other support roles are going on in your school or setting and see if any of these might attract you.
- Discuss with other support staff, role boundary issues and how they can be managed.

What can be done in role boundary disputes?

There are several strategies than can be adopted when faced with a role boundary issue, whether of your own making or others. First is the job description. This needs to be written down and agreed and consulted upon if you or someone else wants to alter it. With that there needs to be an appropriate discussion about rate of pay and redistribution of current roles and responsibilities, and extra training and professional development, so that there is less chance of overloading, resentment, exploitation, or failure. Finally, there needs to be open airing of concerns and an acceptance of the need for support strategies to be put in place to support someone in their exploration of their new role. In the above case, this needs to be achieved by the deployment of a supply teacher for the first week, with Hannah having that time to plan and observe, and consult and co-teach with the supply teacher. The sharing of plans with other Y3 teachers and their overall support and help for her should also be put in place. Ultimately, she shouldn't be used as a supply teacher and, if necessary, she may wish to consult with her union representative or regretfully refuse the task but offer some partial teaching, say in the afternoons for this class, so that the school saves money and she can teach her intervention groups. She would also need to be paid at unqualified teacher rate and her After School Club covered with pay by someone else. Did you agree?

In conclusion

The present Government has, as a result of the economic climate, closed many Children's Centres and Sure Start type facilities, concentrating support only on those supporting the most deprived families. It is also reviewing the role of support staff in schools and inevitable cuts in budgets may see a reversal of the present numbers of support staff in schools. However, the value of support staff in the teaching, learning and caring functions of schools cannot realistically be questioned, though attempts are being made to do so, citing a kind of nostalgic regression to the 1950s where teachers shut doors and taught alone (Harrison, 2011). Now we live in a different world from that of the 1950s. Reverting to an older social model isn't going to work since that model relied on mothers being at home to look after children, teachers being held in fear, and total respect by families and children, and compulsory schooling ending at fifteen, with a host of manual jobs for those who didn't get qualifications, not to mention the pigeon-holing of children by the 11-plus examination into vocational roles, or an academic and professional career, and the segregation of children into special schools and hospitals or homes for the 'ineducable'.

To maintain standards of achievement in the core subjects and support the emotionally vulnerable child, to manage the disruptive pupil and get the school-reluctant to attend, and enable children with SEN to access education, support staff are needed as a central part of the education team.

CHAPTER SUMMARY

This chapter has:

- identified the reasons for an expansion in numbers and types of support staff role in education practice as the growth in inclusion in schools, the application of complex teaching strategies for the core subjects, the pressure to raise achievement in core subjects and GCSEs, the workforce reforms to improve working conditions for teachers, and the development of pastoral support roles as a direct result of the implementation of the *Every Child Matters Agenda* (DfES, 2003);
- identified the differences between support roles and teaching roles, in that the teacher instructs and leads, and the support staff member helps and assists both the teacher in that objective but also the pupils in accessing learning;
- identified that there are vastly different types of jobs in supporting children within education, each carrying a professional and personal level of responsibility, and each subject to the risk of role boundary issues;
- analysed role boundary issues and considered strategies to deal with these that revolve around clarifying job descriptions and lines of responsibility, and developing dialogue and negotiation with appropriate professional support in place when boundaries are stretched.

REFERENCES

Association of Teachers and Lecturers (ATL) and Department for Education and Skills (DfES) et al. (2003) *Raising Standards and Tackling Workloads: A national agreement*, London: DfES.

Department for Education and Employment (DfEE) (1997) *Excellence for all Children: Meeting special educational needs*, London: DfEE.

Department for Education and Employment (DfEE) (1998) *The National Literacy Strategy*, London: DfEE.

Department for Education and Employment (1999), *The National Numeracy Strategy: Framework for teaching mathematics from reception to Year 6*, London: DfEE.

Department for Education and Skills (DfES) (2001) *Special Educational Needs Code of Practice*, London: DfES.

Department for Education and Skills (DfES) (2003) *Every Child Matters Agenda*, London: DfES.

Department for Education and Skills (DfES) (2005) *Excellence and Enjoyment: Social and emotional aspects of learning*, London: DfES.

Edmond, N. and Price, N. (2009) Workforce re-modelling and pastoral care in schools: a diversification of roles or a de-professionalisation of functions? *Pastoral Care in Education*, 27 (4): 301–11.

Goddard, G., Dunne, L, and Woolhouse, C. (2008) Mapping the changes: a critical exploration into the career trajectories of Teaching Assistants who undertake a foundation degree, *Journal of Vocational Education & Training*, 60(1): 49.

Harrison, A. (2011) *Education Bill outlines shake-up for England's Schools*. Available online at www.bbc.co.uk/news/education-12287022 (accessed 13/10/2011).

National Evaluation of Sure Start (NESS) (2002) *Getting Sure Start Started Report NESS/FR/02*. Available online at www.education.gov.uk/publications (accessed 13/10/2011).

Office for Standards in Education (Ofsted) (2008) The deployment, training and development of the wider school workforce, No. HMI 070222. Available online at www.ofsted.gov.uk/resources/deployment-training-and-development-of-the-wider-school-workforce (accessed 13/10/2011).

Plowden Report (1967) *Children and their Primary Schools: A report of the Central Advisory Council for Education (England)*, London: Her Majesty's Stationery Office. Available online at www.educationengland.org.uk/documents/plowden (accessed 13/10/11).

Sykes, J. (ed.) (1975) *The Concise Oxford Dictionary* (6th edition), Oxford: Clarendon Press.

Training and Development Agency for Schools (TDA) (2006a) *HLTA Factsheet for School Leaders and Managers HLTA, Factsheet number 2*. London: TDA.

Training and Development Agency for Schools (TDA) (2006b) *Professional standards for Higher Level Teaching Assistants*. Available online at www.education.gov.uk/publications accessed 13/10/2011).

Training and Development Agency for Schools (TDA) (2008) *Sector Qualification Strategy for School Support Staff*, London: TDA.

Tucker, S. (2009) Perceptions and reflections on the role of the Teaching Assistant in the classroom environment, *Pastoral Care in Education*, 27 (4): 291–300.

2 SUPPORT STAFF AS PROFESSIONALS

Anita Walton

CHAPTER OBJECTIVES

By the end of this chapter you will:

- know how the Teaching Assistant profession has changed;
- understand what is meant by being a professional;
- be able to reflect on the real challenges and dilemmas of professionalism within the workplace.

LINKS TO **HLTA** STANDARDS

1. Have high expectations of children and young people with a commitment to helping them fulfil their potential.

2. Establish fair, respectful, trusting, supportive and constructive relationships with children and young people.

3. Demonstrate the positive values, attitudes and behaviour they expect from children and young people.

4. Communicate effectively and sensitively with children, young people, colleagues, parents and carers.

5. Recognise and respect the contribution that parents and carers can make to the development and well-being of children and young people.

6. Demonstrate a commitment to collaborative and co-operative working with colleagues.

7. Improve their own knowledge and practice, including responding to advice and feedback.

Introduction

This chapter will look at how the Teaching Assistant (TA) role as a professional has grown and developed over the past few years. It will give you time to reflect on what is meant by being a professional in a work context and it will explore some of the challenges and dilemmas that can face you when working with a team of professionals and with children and parents.

The development of the profession

If you have been working within the school environment for a while, take a few minutes to think about how things have changed in relation to the work and role of TAs. If you are relatively new to this role you might like to ask more experienced colleagues about this.

In recent years there have been an increasing number of TAs in both primary and secondary schools.

- There was a 97 per cent increase in the number of support staff between 1997 and 2005, from 136,500 to 268,600.
- This compares with only an 8 per cent increase in the number of teachers over the same period.
- DfES figures suggest one of the fastest-growing groups over this period is that of the TA, with numbers rising from 61,300 to 148,500 (TDA, 2006). The DfE figure for TAs at November 2010 was 229,900 (DfE, 2011).

There has also been a change in role and responsibilities. These changes are partly a result of education reform in the 1980s, which followed the Warnock Report of 1978 when the number of TAs was increased specifically to work with pupils with special educational needs (SEN).

There was a growing concern in the late 1990s that a number of reforms had increased the workload and accountability of teachers. The Department for Education and Skills (DfES) commissioned PriceWaterhouseCoopers (2001) to undertake an investigation into teacher workload, which led to a policy to remodel the workforce (DfES, 2003). According to Mansaray (2006, p172):

> The authors of the report recommended more innovative deployment of support staff to take over administrative tasks. TAs would be encouraged to take on greater teaching roles, allowing teachers guaranteed non-contact time for planning, preparation and assessment (PPA) and reduced workloads.

In 2001, Estelle Morris, who was then Secretary of State for Education, announced at a speech to the Social Market Foundation that:

> Teaching Assistants will be
> - supervising classes that are undertaking work set by a teacher, or working with small groups of pupils on reading practice;
> - supervising lunchtime activities and invigilating tests;
> - giving pastoral and other individual support to pupils, and covering for teacher absence;
> - spending more of their time on teaching, lesson preparation, assessing individual pupil progress and updating their professional skills.
>
> (Morris, 2001, p16)

Workforce reform, following the Workforce Agreement (DfES, 2003) meant that duties previously carried out by teachers would be passed on to support staff. These duties included planning and taking whole classes. The Higher Level Teaching Assistant (HLTA) status was introduced in which TAs were assessed against standards very similar to those of the Qualified

Teacher status (DfES/TTA, 2003). These policies and developing practices led towards a professionalisation of teaching assistants; however, TAs in general had few professional development opportunities that allowed them to acquire reflective strategies (Lee, 2002). Continuing professional development (CPD) tended to be focused on teachers rather than TAs. Potter and Richardson agreed with this view, and commented that, while teachers are expected to evaluate their own practice, little attention had been given to the needs of classroom assistants to develop critical reflection skills:

> Given the increasingly educational role of classroom assistants in both mainstream and special schools, there is a need to ensure that they become reflective practitioners within classroom teams.
>
> (1999, p36)

In 2004 the remit of the Training and Development Agency (TDA) for schools was enhanced to include responsibility for the training and development of the wider school workforce, so that the whole school team could work together for standards to be raised (TDA, 2005). In 2006 the TDA published a three-year strategy for support staff training and development. TAs are now aware that there is an emphasis on training and professional development for them so that their role can be developed even further. The strategy has three main objectives.

1. *Support schools as they develop new ways of training and deploying their support staff.*
2. *Create a framework of standards and qualifications to enable schools to develop the potential of all support staff.*
3. *Extend training opportunities to meet the development needs of all support staff.*

(TDA, 2006, p9)

What is meant by 'professional'?

The term 'professional' crops up in many phrases and has a variety of meanings. Phrases used include: 'being a professional', 'education professional', 'professional development' and 'behaving professionally'.

> **REFLECTIVE TASK**
>
> What do you think is meant by the term 'professional?' List the key words and phrases that you come up with.

Characteristics of being professional

Respect

Being professional involves being respectful to all staff, pupils, parents and colleagues. Professionals should foster an atmosphere of mutual respect. Your behaviour to pupils should be such that the pupil understands that they are respected and valued. You can do this by:

- communicating in a way that they will be able to understand, which may be different for varying age groups and pupils who have difficulties in communicating;
- being fair and inclusive;

- using positive language;
- supporting pupils to show respect in their communication with each other.

> **REFLECTIVE TASK**
> In what other ways can you show pupils that you respect and value them?

Confidentiality

As a professional, you will also need to respect the confidentiality of information relating to pupils. You may have seen information on Individual Education Plans (IEPs) and marks and levels relating to their work.

You may have access to, or knowledge of, sensitive information about pupils and it is imperative that this information remains confidential. Sometimes you would not even share this information with colleagues if they have no reason to be aware of it. Always check before divulging any information about a pupil to colleagues and take great care that you always respect confidentiality. You may divulge something inadvertently during a casual conversation or you may think that someone already knows, so always be vigilant.

> CASE STUDY 1
> *Josie Springer works at Rosemary Street Primary School as a TA. Last Saturday, in the supermarket, one of her pupils' parents approached her and asked how she thought Stephen was doing in his reading. Josie replied 'He is on level 6 and doing really well; he's one of the best readers in the class, and has even overtaken George.' On Monday, George's father demanded to speak to the class teacher and complained that confidential information about his son's reading level was given to a parent.*

In this case study, Josie did act unprofessionally as she should not have discussed another pupil's work or level with Stephen's parents. This case study shows how difficult it is to know what to say when approached in an informal setting. Clearly, Josie did not have access to pupil records at the supermarket, and should she have said anything without discussing it with the teacher?

> **REFLECTIVE TASK**
> In case study 1, how do you think Josie should have responded to Stephen's parent?

> CASE STUDY 2
> *Peter is a special needs support assistant who works with a Year 5 boy called Danny, who has emotional and behavioural difficulties. Peter has formed a very close relationship with Danny and his family. Prior to a review meeting, Peter read a very negative report about Danny's progress written by the SENCO. It concluded with a strong recommendation for removal to a special school. Concerned that Danny's parents would be taken by surprise at the review meeting by this report, he photocopied it and sent it anonymously to the parents.*

In this case study Peter acted unprofessionally. His concern for Danny's parents was no excuse for him divulging this information.

REFLECTIVE TASK
Looking at case study 2, what do you think are the potential consequences of Peter's actions for Peter, for the school and for Danny?

Professional conduct and behaviour in school

Respecting colleagues

Being a professional in school involves conducting yourself in a professional manner. This involves working collaboratively with colleagues and respecting their professional expertise. Sometimes it will be a specialist who you will have to work with, such as a social worker or a speech and language therapist, rather than a teacher, and you will need to make sure that you understand and follow any instructions. If you are not sure what you are meant to do, ask them to explain it to you.

Part of being a professional means having a professional approach at all times and being careful about all conversations you have when in earshot of the pupils.

CASE STUDY 3
Two TAs, Jane and Stephen, were in a study support area where pupils were engaged in independent research. Jane said to Stephen, 'I'm not looking forward to the next class, I've got Mrs Taylor doing history and she hasn't got a clue about the kids and her lessons are always boring.'

Sometimes professionals working in schools make judgements about other professionals in a casual conversation. This could be viewed as being unprofessional. In this case study, Jane was clearly acting unprofessionally as she could be heard by the pupils. Instead, she should have thought about her role in the lesson and how she could work with the teacher to have a positive impact on the lesson.

REFLECTIVE TASK
Looking at case study 3, how would you respond if you were Stephen?

Voicing concerns

Most of the time teachers and TAs are clear about their roles in the classroom. In the real world, however, TAs may be asked to undertake work they do not feel confident about. In these circumstances you must voice your concerns and ask for advice. State clearly exactly what it is that you are concerned about and why. Voicing your concerns does not mean that you are being unprofessional. Being part of a professional team means that you are able to discuss situations and problems that are difficult for you.

CASE STUDY 4

Susan is a secondary school general TA working across all departments. The head of the ICT department had set up a lesson in the ICT room involving researching on the internet for a personal project with Year 8. Susan was assisting the ICT teacher who, halfway through the lesson, told her that he was feeling ill, and could she monitor the class and dismiss them at the end of the lesson. Susan is a relatively new TA employed at level 2 and she didn't feel she could take this class, but was frightened of getting into trouble, so she agreed. Towards the end of the lesson she noticed that some of the class had managed to access an internet chat room, and were giggling and posting messages. She asked them to close down the site and return to their work, but they refused.

In this case study, Susan should have told the teacher that she didn't feel confident to take the class on her own and asked if she could send one of the pupils to the office so that someone could be sent to cover the lesson. Sometimes not voicing concerns earlier enough can cause more problems later on.

Dress code

According to research by Fortenberry et al. (1978), Forsythe et al. (1984) and Kim and Lennon (2005), the clothes we wear can have a significant influence on how we are perceived by others. Dress can convey personal characteristics, such as decisiveness and authoritativeness. Dressing smartly suggests that we respect our position as a professional.

Most schools would expect clothing:

- to be clean;
- not to be shabby;
- to be properly fitting;
- not to look sloppy;
- to be appropriate for the setting;
- not to have slogans or represent a particular following.

Take a few minutes to think about why dressing in a certain way matters. What messages are received by children, young people, parents and other professionals when we dress professionally? Ask your colleagues what they think would be professional dress. Do they think the type of clothes you wear in school is important in the way you are perceived by staff, pupils and parents?

Timekeeping

I have always been a quarter of an hour before my time, and it has made a man of me.

(Lord Nelson)

TAs need to provide good models of behaviour to pupils by organising and managing their activities responsibly and effectively while practising good timekeeping. Punctuality does not just apply to first thing in the morning when you arrive at school. It applies after breaks and lunch, and being punctual for each lesson. It is very disrespectful to be late without a good reason, and your late arrival in the classroom could interrupt others while they are talking.

It can, however, be very difficult to arrive in plenty of time to undertake your work, particularly if you have to move from one side of the building to the other.

> **PRACTICAL TASK**
> Consider your own timekeeping. Are there any ways you could improve this? Make a list of recommendations for yourself and try them out, and discuss stress points with the key professionals concerned.

Language and non-verbal communication

As professionals, TAs will be expected to communicate using acceptable language. Unacceptable language would include:

- swearing;
- negative language;
- language that is disrespectful;
- inappropriate language of a sexual nature;
- language that is racist, sexist or disrespectful to a religion.

Discuss with colleagues what is and is not acceptable language to use in your work environment. Is there a difference between communicating with staff and with children or young people? Explore why codes of language are important to professionalism.

We communicate to others through body language as well as words. In some ways this posturing is more powerful than speech. According to Mehrabian (1971) there are three elements to communication: spoken words, tone of voice and body language. In his research he determined the following generalisations.

- 7 per cent of communication happens in spoken words.
- 38 per cent of communication happens through voice tone.
- 55 per cent of communication happens via general body language.

CASE STUDY 5

Paul is a Year 7 pupil who wanted to get his bag out of his form room at lunchtime as his lunch was in it. David, a Year 11 pupil, stood in front of the classroom door so that Paul couldn't get in. Paul asked to go into the classroom. David crossed his arms, stared at the pupil for about ten seconds, and then said 'I don't think so.' Paul asked again if he could go into the classroom, but David just shrugged his shoulders and stared at him again. Paul looked upset and walked away without his lunch.

In this case study, David, by staring, was conveying an aggressive attitude and crossing his arms showed that he wasn't going to move. Shrugging his shoulders conveyed that he didn't care about what Paul wanted.

PRACTICAL TASK

Spend some time now identifying postures that would be considered as being unfriendly, uninterested, bored or frightened. Look out for these in the workplace environment. Pupils may be good sources for this. Think about how negative body language can have an impact on your pupils, your colleagues and other professionals?

Now think about how we can convey interest, enthusiasm, openness, assertiveness and confidence through body language. Practise these in front of a mirror. Become more aware of your body language and start to incorporate positive posturing and stances.

Suggestions for professional conduct in school

- Make sure you are aware of the expected professional code of dress for the school.
- Make sure you are always on time for lessons, duties or meetings.
- Try to be positive in your language and your non-verbal communication.

Involvement in the school

Being a professional also means being involved in whole-school matters and staff meetings. You will also need an awareness of school organisational needs and sensitivity to pupil and staff needs. You may also need subject expertise and skills when working with certain pupils or classes.

As a TA you will be working as a member of a professional team or several professional teams and you will probably be taking on several roles. You will need to know when to use your initiative, when to seek advice, when to speak and when not to. If you are liaising with other professionals outside school, you will need good communication skills and an understanding of your role within that team. In Chapter 3 you will learn more about working in partnership with other professionals.

PRACTICAL TASK

What kind of professional skills and attitudes would be required when working with the following shown in table opposite? Copy and complete the table opposite (the first one has been done for you).

Challenges

Why is it sometimes difficult to act professionally?

- Sometimes it is difficult if you are dealing with aggression or unfairness from pupils, parents or staff. You may want to retaliate, but that wouldn't help.
- Some TAs may lack confidence to participate in or contribute to meetings.
- Sometimes it is difficult to be positive if you are not feeling very well.

REFLECTIVE TASK

What do you think are the challenges to acting professionally?

WORKING WITH	PROFESSIONAL SKILLS
Parents	We would expect TAs working with parents to respect the confidentiality of all pupils and staff and to be polite at all times. TAs would be required to know when, and to whom, to refer any issues beyond their sphere of competence.
Teachers	
Multi-agency teams	
After-school clubs	
Whole-school staff meetings	
Small-group settings	
Whole-class settings	
An individual child	
School governors	

HLTA standards for professional values and practice

The list below shows the HLTA standards that are concerned with professional attributes.

Here is an example for the first standard.

Example
I run an after-school club for Year 7 and 8 pupils who are having difficulty in maths lessons. We use maths games on the computer and I try to give lots of individual feedback and praise. The Year 7 and 8 maths teachers have told me that the pupils are now more confident in their maths lessons and are answering questions. At the end of the year, the National Curriculum level has improved in maths for nearly all those who attended the club.

PRACTICAL TASK
First read through these standards and reflect on your own practice. Choose two of the standards and give examples of how you meet each standard.

Professional attributes

Those awarded HLTA status must demonstrate, through their practice, that they:

1. Have high expectations of children and young people with a commitment to helping them fulfil their potential.
   - Demonstrate how you encourage pupils to raise their achievement through increased participation in learning activities.
   - Identify barriers to pupils' participating and achieving and minimise these barriers.
   - Challenge stereotypical views and low expectations of what pupils can achieve.

2. Establish fair, respectful, trusting, supportive and constructive relationships with children and young people.
   - Become familiar with school policies and classroom rules and routines to ensure that pupils are treated in a consistent manner.
   - Treat pupils in ways that promote a positive self-image and develop self-esteem and explain reasons for any actions or consequences, taking care not to embarrass them.
   - Take an interest in pupils' preferences and attitudes, listen to them and involve them equally in activities.

3. Demonstrate the positive values, attitudes and behaviour they expect from children and young people.
   - Model courteous modes of address and address any name-calling, rudeness or thoughtlessness and inappropriate treatment of property and buildings.
   - Remind pupils of school policies and classroom protocols concerning rights and responsibilities and be familiar with such policies.
   - Deal with subject content that enables promotion of positive values, attitudes and behaviour, e.g. circle time, topic work, PSHE, citizenship, history, literature, educational visits and assembly preparation.
   - Promote a community among groups of pupils from mixed ethnic backgrounds.

4. Communicate effectively and sensitively with children, young people, colleagues, parents and carers.
   - Vary the style of communication depending on the purpose, face-to-face, telephone or written.
   - Be sensitive to variations in family values and practices across and within cultural groupings, and avoid assumptions and judgements about parents and carers.
   - Know school policies and procedures.
   - Understand confidentiality requirements, knowing what information to pass on and to whom.
   - Maintain effective boundaries between roles as a member of a community and as a member of school staff.
   - Brief teachers with information about pupils' motivation, behaviour and attainment that teachers can use in reporting to parents.

5. Recognise and respect the contribution that parents and carers can make to the development and well-being of children and young people.
   - Keep parents and carers informed of matters relating to their child.
   - Engage with parents and carers in understanding the needs of the child.
   - Involve parents and carers in children's learning.

6. Demonstrate a commitment to collaborative and co-operative working with colleagues.
   - Demonstrate how your participation in the team contributes to taking forward pupils' learning.
   - Demonstrate that you can take the initiative and make decisions in the context of teachers' guidance and the school's policies and practice.
   - Know when and from whom to seek advice and support.
   - Be aware of issues beyond the scope of your role and refer these to colleagues as appropriate.

7. Improve their own knowledge and practice, including responding to advice and feedback.
   - Demonstrate that you can acquire new knowledge and skills, e.g. training course, e-learning, reading, discussion with colleagues and other professionals.
   - Demonstrate how you acquired new knowledge and then use this to take pupils' learning forward.
   - Review and modify your own practice as a result of observation or discussion.
   - Demonstrate that you carry out realistic self-evaluation and that you respond to and act upon feedback, e.g. setting targets.
   - Improve your own practice on own initiative or through the school CPD arrangements.

(adapted from TDA, 2007)

CHAPTER SUMMARY

- The TA professional has grown and developed over the last few years.
- There are real challenges and dilemmas of professionalism within the workplace.
- You should now be able to reflect on what is meant by being a professional in a work context.

REFERENCES

Department for Education (DfE) (2011) DfE: *School Workforce in England, November 2010 (Provisional)*. Available online at www.education.gov.uk/rsgateway/DB/SFR/s000997/index.shtml (accessed 31/10/2011).

Department for Education and Skills (DfES) (2003) *Developing the Role of School Support Staff*. London: DFES.

Department for Education and Skills (DfES)/Teacher Training Agency (TTA) (2003) *Professional Standards for Higher Level Teaching Assistants*. London: DfES/TTA.

Forsythe, S., Drake, M. and Cox, C. (1984) Dress as an influence on the perceptions of management characteristics in women. *Family and Consumer Sciences Research Journal*, 13(2): 112–21.

Fortenberry, J., MacLean, J., Morris, P. and O'Connell, M. (1978) Mode of dress as a perceptual cue to deference. *Journal of Social Psychology*, 104: 139–40.

Kim, M. and Lennon, S. (2005) The effects of customers' dress on salespersons' service in large-sized clothing specialty stores. *Clothing and Textiles Research Journal*, 23(2): 78–87.

Lee, C. (2002) *Teaching Assistants in Schools: The current state of play*. London: NFER.

Mansaray, A. (2006) Liminality and in/exclusion: exploring the work of teaching assistants. *Pedagogy, Culture & Society*, 14: 171–87.

Mehrabian, A. (1971) *Silent Messages*. Wadsworth, CA: Belmont.

Morris, E. (2001) *Professionalism and Trust: The future of teachers and teaching*. Speech to the Social Market Foundation, 29 November.

PriceWaterhouseCoopers (2001) *Teacher Workload Study: Final report*. London: DfES.

Potter, C. A. and Richardson, H. L. (1999) Facilitating classroom assistants' professional reflection through video workshops. *British Journal of Special Education*, 26(1): 34–6.

Training and Development Agency (TDA) (2005) *Building the School Team*. Available online at www.education.gov.uk/publications/eOrderingDownload/TEA0500.pdf (accessed 1/3/2012).

Training and Development Agency (TDA) (2006) *Developing People to Support Learning: A skills strategy for the wider school workforce 2006–09*. Available online at http://dera.ioe.ac.uk/6429/1/swdb_3ys.pdf (accessed 1/3/2012).

Training and Development Agency (TDA) (2007) *Higher Level Teaching Assistants*. Available online at www.tda.gov.uk/cpd-leader/standards-qualifications/professional-standards/-/media/resources/support-staff/hlta/tda0425hlta-the-way-forward.pdf (accessed 1/3/2012).

FURTHER READING

Rose, R. (2005) *Becoming a Primary Higher Level Teaching Assistant*. Exeter: Learning Matters.

3 WORKING WITH OTHER PROFESSIONALS

Susan Graves

CHAPTER OBJECTIVES

By the end of this chapter you will:

- be able to discuss a number of strategies and initiatives that have impacted on the development of the children's workforce in schools;
- appreciate how integrated assessment and inspection frameworks are impacting on the development of integrated working;
- understand how an integrated children's workforce is developing;
- appreciate the benefits and challenges of multi-agency, multi-professional working and some of the skills needed for successful team working.

LINKS TO **HLTA** STANDARDS

1. Communicate effectively and sensitively with children, young people, colleagues, parents and carers.
2. Demonstrate a commitment to collaborative and co-operative working with colleagues.
3. Know how other frameworks, which support the development and well-being of children and young people, impact upon their practice.
4. Contribute to maintaining and analysing records of learners' progress.
5. Direct the work, where relevant, of other adults in supporting learning.

Introduction

This chapter will look at the development of an integrated workforce as a key aspect of the previous government's strategy for the provision of children's services in the UK. It will look at the benefits and challenges of multi-agency, multi-professional working in the development of an integrated children's workforce. Additionally, it will examine how the development of an Integrated Qualifications Framework (IQF) and Common Core of Skills and Knowledge for this workforce is intended to align professionals' work more collaboratively. The development of children's centres and extended schools will also be discussed, along with the Common Assessment and Integrated Inspection Frameworks that are intended to ensure that services move away from being professional silos, and become interdependent and inter-reliant in terms of monitoring and improving children's services.

Developing the school workforce

Background

The reform of the school workforce was part of a larger agenda intended to develop integrated services for children. The intention is that services, in terms of education, health and social services, will be offered in a more cohesive manner to children and their families, possibly from a single site. Developments also include increasing provision for children and families through extended schools, expanding the school curriculum to offer choice and diversity to pupils, the introduction of more personalised learning, and changes to testing and examinations at all levels.

These developments inevitably mean changes to the way in which schools operate and to the roles of those who work in them. Change is an inevitable part of the lives of organisations in the twenty-first century and nowhere is this more in evidence than in the educational world. Government initiatives and policies in the years 2000–2012 have seen some of the most radical changes in the way schools are managed and funded, in the design, delivery and testing of the curriculum and in the profile of staff working within the classroom. For those working in schools, the ability to adapt and deal with this change from both professional and personal points of view is vital.

From the perspective of schools, it is those schools that are able to adopt and adapt new initiatives to their own context, grasp opportunities to enhance funding, for example through special funding grants, and maximise the potential of the whole workforce, that will be able to survive and thrive in the future.

Developing support staff

The development of support staff in schools was a key feature of the previous Labour government's remodelling agenda, with the twin aims of enhancing learning within the classroom and ensuring that the changes to teachers' contracts – designed to enhance their work/life balance and give time within the school day for preparation, planning and assessment – are implemented within every school. This was set out in the National Workforce Agreement, which was signed by ministers on 15 January 2003. This is a national agreement with key partners, including local authority employers and some school workforce unions, which laid out statutory contractual conditions under which teachers would be employed with a view to a progressive reduction in teachers' overall hours. A timetable for implementation was included, which gave deadlines for instigating a concerted attack on unnecessary paperwork and bureaucratic processes, additional resources and a national change management programme and reform of support staff roles (DfES, 2003a).

PRACTICAL TASK

Do your own research on the National Workforce Agreement – a starting point is the Department for Education website at www.education.gov.uk/schools

The National Workforce Agreement

The agreement was informed by the Teacher Workload study, which had been undertaken by PriceWaterhouseCoopers and reported in December 2001 (PWC, 2001). This study looked at workloads for teachers and other staff in schools nationally and made recommendations for future staffing policy in schools based on the research. The recommendations included strategies to reduce teachers' overall working hours by deploying support staff in more enhanced roles within classrooms alongside the introduction of guaranteed non-contact time for teachers. They foresaw the latter being managed through a *mix of increased use of supply staff; recruitment of additional teaching staff; supporting learning through staff other than teachers; and/or supporting learning using ICT* (PWC, 2001, p105). They acknowledged within the report that using support staff in enhanced classroom roles was of concern to many on educational grounds and, though they were broadly supportive of the introduction of the para-professional role for support staff, agreed that *the rationale [for using support staff in the classroom] must clearly be established on grounds of quality and on better use of staffing resources* (PWC, 2001, p44).

A publication from Ofsted, *Workforce reform in schools – has it made a difference?* published in January 2010, was based on a survey conducted between May 2008 and March 2009 in 30 English schools. Inspectors visited 16 primary schools and 14 secondary schools to evaluate how effectively workforce reform had been implemented and to assess whether it had made a difference to the quality of teaching, to pupils' learning and to outcomes for pupils and their families. The key features in the schools visited that enabled members of the wider workforce to make a difference to pupils' learning included:

- *collaborative planning and good-quality direction from teachers, ensuring that members of the wider workforce were directly involved in supporting teaching and learning and in assessing and recording pupils' progress;*
- *a shared understanding by staff of what constituted good teaching and learning and effective support for these activities;*
- *careful monitoring of pupils' progress after intervention programmes, ensuring that improvement was consolidated and sustained in the classroom;*
- *consistent evaluation of interventions for disaffected and/or vulnerable pupils, undertaken across all key stages;*
- *a coherent programme of high-quality curriculum support and extended provision that related clearly to teachers' work and focused on extending and enriching pupils' learning.*

(Ofsted, 2010)

The key findings of the report indicated that the most effective schools were ones where leaders deployed staff well and gave clear direction in terms of professional status and accountability. In these schools all members of the workforce understood how they contributed to pupil learning and had a clear understanding of their own roles and those of others. In this respect collaborative planning between teachers and support staff, and a shared understanding of what constitutes good teaching and assessment, led to more effective classroom support and intervention. The report also suggests that support staff with qualifications and training specific to their role were shown to produce high quality interventions and outcomes and that support staff could provide useful links with parents and the wider community. However, the report does highlight that the majority of the school leaders and staff included in the survey had little knowledge of the National Occupational Standards for Support Staff or the Career Development Framework

(TDA, 2007), which reduced the opportunities for coherent career planning and professional development for support staff and prevented the cultivation of their professional status.

REFLECTIVE TASK

Read the report at www.ofsted.gov.uk/node/2409 – Workforce reform in schools: has it made a difference? Consider the examples of good practice described and how these may be utilised in your school.

Other national drivers

There are other national drivers that are significant in developing an enhanced role for support staff in schools. The policy of the previous government was focused on the concept of universality in terms of education funding, that is, the focus is on all children, best demonstrated by the *Every Child Matters* (ECM) policy. Other features of this approach included the establishment of Children's Centres in local neighbourhoods which could be accessed by all, regardless of need, and the introduction of extended schools providing services for all children in the local community outside normal school times. Alongside these developments primary schools were encouraged to enhance the school curriculum to offer a broad and varied mix, secondary schools were required to increase the take-up of sporting opportunities for pupils and schools were encouraged to develop as specialist schools and colleges, which attracted enhanced funding (DfES, 2002).

All of the above initiatives inevitably had an effect on the staffing policies within schools with an experienced and well-qualified support staff needed to support teachers and others to deliver the extended services outlined. Indeed, in the ten-year period from 1997 to 2007 the number of support staff working in schools increased exponentially and now forms more than half of the total school workforce.

The formation of the coalition government in 2010 signalled a change in emphasis in terms of policy and the Spending Review in October 2010 announced a more targeted approach to funding steered towards those children and families in most need together with an end to ring-fencing of school budgets to give individual schools the freedom to pursue their own priorities in line with local need. Alongside these changes proposals in the Special Educational Needs (SEN) and Disability Green Paper (DfE, 2011a) advocate a single education, health and care plan for individuals from birth to 25 years of age with budgets held by parents or carers who will be able to choose the services which they feel best suit their need. The role of voluntary and community sector organisations is seen as a key element of the proposals as well as a strong partnership between all local services and agencies. It is unclear how these changes will impact on support staff in schools, but the focus of the Higher Level Teaching Assistant status in more specialised areas such as Maths, Science and Food Technology, together with the end to ring-fencing of funds for professional development, may signal a change of direction in this respect. For more information about the professional development of support staff go to www.tda.gov.uk and for the SEN Green Paper, visit www.education.gov.uk/schools. Below is a case study which demonstrates how one school developed a culture in which TAs could explore development and deployment issues, identify possible solutions and share them with the senior leadership team.

CASE STUDY: THE CHERWELL SCHOOL: OXFORD

Challenges
- *To create a sustainable model through which Teaching Assistants (TAs) can work in equal partnership with teachers.*
- *To increase TA profile and confidence.*
- *To ensure consistency of TA access to training and continuing professional development (CPD) opportunities.*

What the school did
- *Held workshops through which TAs could explore development and deployment issues, identify possible solutions and share them with the senior leadership team.*
- *Created a plan through which solutions could be implemented.*

Outcomes
- *There has been an immediate improvement in communications between TAs and teachers.*
- *TAs have gained confidence and have better working relationships with teachers.*
- *TAs have identified issues which are preventing them being effective in the classroom; have suggested how to measure the difference they make to pupil learning and have drafted proposals about how to implement changes throughout the school. Local authority (LA) funding has been secured to embed the work started at Cherwell across the LA.*
- *The school will be evaluating the impact on pupil progress.*

(adapted from TDA website www.tda.gov.uk/school-leader/effective-staff-deployment/effective-deployment-of-school-leaders/case-studies/cherwell.aspx)

REFLECTIVE TASK
- Would your school benefit from the above approach? In what ways?
- Look back at the Ofsted Report (2010) mentioned previously, does the above approach fit with their recommendations of how all staff should work together?
- What would be the benefits to pupils of this approach?

The 14–19 agenda

The numbers of young people not in education, employment or training (known as NEETs) in the 14–19 bracket have been of concern to the government in recent years. In an effort to address this concern, major reforms to education and training for 14–19-year-olds were first set out in February 2005 in *14–19 Education and Skills* (DCSF, 2005), which was followed by a 14–19 implementation plan in December of the same year. Some modifications and developments to the initial proposals followed, culminating in a new consultation document in March 2008, *Promoting Achievement, Valuing Success: A strategy for 14–19 qualifications* (DCSF, 2008).

The strategy advocates a new broad curriculum for the 14–19-year-old age group, which includes vocational pathways delivered through flexible, integrated programmes that young people can access through a variety of providers. There are also proposals for clear vocational pathways to higher education to be developed that would give young people undertaking work-related programmes and apprenticeships a clear progression to degree programmes, which will extend their practical competence and also give a sound academic underpinning (DCSF, 2008). In 2011 the Wolf Report continued this theme of advocating a broad curriculum for young people but suggested that young people should not be allowed to specialise too early and those who reached the end of Key Stage 4 with weak English and Maths should continue with them. The report advocates per student funding for post-16 provision, rather than the individual qualification funding which had applied previously, in order to encourage providers to develop coherent programmes of study for this age group. Alongside this recommendation the report suggests that a more relaxed attitude should prevail in terms of the development of specialist provision, a move away from the prescriptive rigidity of the past. Wolf suggests that in this way more providers will be enabled to offer highly distinctive and high quality provision for young people. This is in line with government policy to develop more specialist provision through University Technical Colleges, Academies and Free Schools, which are publicly funded but privately run.

PRACTICAL TASK

Look at the Wolf Report on vocational Education (2011b) at www.education.gov. uk/publications/standard/publicationDetail/Page1/DFE-00038-2011

Also look at the Schools White Paper *The Importance of Teaching* (2010) at www.education.gov.uk/publications/standard/publicationDetail/Page1/CM%207980

Make a list of the staff who are potentially involved in successfully delivering this strategy for young people at the local level.

We can see, if we reflect on the above, that the role of enhanced support staff in schools supporting teachers with these initiatives plays a crucial part in linking together the various agencies and staff who will be working towards ensuring the best possible outcomes for pupils. In these circumstances, the staffing policy of the whole school needs to be examined to ensure that the necessary skills and experience are developed across the whole workforce in terms of access to professional and career development.

It also has to be acknowledged that there is some distrust and disquiet within the teaching profession concerning the enhanced role of support staff that has emerged as a result of workforce reform in schools. This is particularly apparent concerning the interface of the role of the teacher and TAs, whose duties may have a great deal of overlap. Some teachers feel that the profession has had to work hard to ensure an all-graduate teaching force and to keep pupil/teacher ratio within reasonable limits. There is suspicion that although guidance to schools is very clear, assistants are required to work under the direct supervision of a qualified teacher and in practice this does not always happen (Stevenson, 2007). Furthermore, there is some concern in terms of the emergence of schools outside direct local control (academies, free schools, etc.) which are able to employ staff outside national agreements and that unqualified staff may be used to replace teachers on a much lower salary and with less favourable terms and conditions of work. This issue of professionalism and how overlapping and new roles are managed in the change process makes us realise that at the heart of this remodelling agenda people are sometimes having to make painful and difficult adjustments to their own perceptions of their professional role.

REFLECTIVE TASK

List some of the challenges and benefits in terms of developing the role of support staff within the school workforce.

Developing an integrated children's workforce

This section looks at some of the issues in developing an integrated workforce for children.

Background

The concept of an integrated workforce for children's services is, in part, a result of the Laming Report (2003), which reported on the Victoria Climbié scandal. This report has had an important impact on children's policy, as the findings identified serious failures in the lack of communication and collaboration between professionals across healthcare, education, police and social services, which, it was felt, resulted in the tragic death of the five-year-old.

The Every Child Matters Agenda

A major initiative of the last Labour government to address these issues was *Every Child Matters: Change for children* (DfES) (2003b), with its five aims:

> *that every child, whatever their background or their circumstances, will have the support they need to:*
> - *Be healthy*
> - *Stay safe*
> - *Enjoy and achieve*
> - *Make a positive contribution*
> - *Achieve economic well-being*
>
> (DfES, 2003a)

This is informing the structure and operation of the new children's services in terms of policy, service provision and workforce education. To develop a workforce that will be able to meet the requirements of the ECM policy, the *Children's Workforce Strategy* set out the requirements in terms of developing a workforce that:

> - *strives to achieve the best possible outcomes for all children and young people;*
> - *is competent, confident and safe to work with children and young people;*
> - *[people] aspire to be part of and want to remain in – where they can develop their skills and build satisfying and rewarding careers; and*
> - *parents, children and young people trust and respect.*
>
> (DfES, 2005a, p6)

Common Core of Skills and Knowledge

To help an integrated children's workforce to work together in a consistent and proficient way, a Common Core of Skills and Knowledge has been devised as a requirement for all those working with children. The Common Core has been identified as detailed below.

- Effective communication and engagement with children and young people.
- Child and young person development.
- Safeguarding and promoting the welfare of the child.
- Supporting transitions.
- Multi-agency working.
- Sharing information.

The idea is that all qualifications for those working within the children's workforce would contain the above elements with a common purpose and language. An Integrated Qualifications Framework (IQF) was introduced in 2008, in which all qualifications for those working within the children's workforce will be placed. The development of the Common Core may also allow for progression and transfer of staff between sectors, and a better sharing of knowledge and practice across sectors.

Common Assessment Framework

The Common Assessment Framework (CAF) is a standardised approach to conducting an assessment of a child's additional needs and deciding how those needs should be met. It can be used by practitioners from all disciplines who have contact with the child and the intention is that it will promote more effective, earlier identification of additional needs, particularly in universal services. It is intended to provide a simple process for a holistic assessment of a child's needs and strengths, taking account of the roles of parents, carers and environmental factors in their development. Practitioners will then be better placed to agree, with the child and the family, about what support is appropriate. The CAF will also help to improve integrated working by promoting co-ordinated service provision.

Children's centres

Children's centres provide integrated services to children under five and their families, from the antenatal period until children start in reception or Year 1 at primary school. Centres may also offer other services, such as training for parents in terms of parenting classes, basic skills classes or training for work sessions. The intention is that parents will be able to access all the services they may need to support them through the centre and in this way the needs of families can be met in the local community.

Extended schools

The DCSF document, *Extended Schools: Building on experience* (2005b), sets out a core offer of services that all children will be able to access through schools by 2010.

The core offer includes:

- a varied range of activities, including study support, sport and music clubs, combined with childcare in primary schools;

- parenting and family support;
- swift and easy access to targeted and specialist services;
- community access to facilities, including adult and family learning, ICT and sports grounds.

It is intended that schools will work closely with parents, children and others to shape these activities around the needs of their community and may choose to provide extra services in response to demand.

Integrated Inspection Framework

The proposals set out under the previous labour government in the ECM Green Paper and in the Children Act 2004 prompted new arrangements for the inspection of children's services at local authority area level. Integrated inspections of children's services replaced inspections of individual services and it was hoped that they would act as a driver to develop joint ways of working within local areas. Services are monitored through two inspection processes: an annual performance assessment (APA) of each council's children's service; and a programme of joint area reviews (JARs), which involve greater depth than the APA and also range beyond council services to include, for example, health and police services. Both processes are intended to look at how services are working together locally to improve outcomes for children and young people.

In October 2011 the coalition government announced that £10.5m would be made available in 2011/12 to support the development and implementation of a new system of improvement and challenge in children's services. This will be led by local authority children's services through a Children's Improvement Board, membership of which will initially include local government representatives – the Association of Directors of Children's Services (ADCS), the Local Government Group (LGG), the Society of Local Authority Chief Executives – and the Department for Education.

It is widely agreed that LAs will own and deliver the new system, which will work on the basis of:

- an assessment based on self-evaluation, peer review and challenge, underpinned by a streamlined inspection regime;
- a range of improvement offers that are brokered, commissioned and (mostly) delivered by the sector, and that rely on good use of evidence;
- capacity-building support as LAs shift increasingly towards being strategic commissioners – working with the voluntary and community sector and other partners to deliver services;
- coordinated support for LAs as new policies and priorities are implemented.

It is hoped that this more open and transparent approach across local authorities will reduce instances of failure, and the most significant shift is in the emphasis on local authority's freedom to shape services to suit their local situations. Additionally, there is a general move from government towards local authorities becoming commissioners rather than deliverers of services; in other words, using the voluntary and private sector to provide services previously undertaken by staff employed directly by the local authority.

This theme of the localised development of services was also evident in the *Munro Review of Child Protection*, which was published in May 2011 and which suggested that local areas should have more freedom to develop their own child protection services, rather than focusing on meeting central government targets. The report concludes that a one-size-fits-all approach to child protection is preventing local areas from focusing on the child and that previous reforms, while well-intentioned, resulted in a tick-box culture and a loss of focus on the needs of the child. The report suggests that currently local areas are judged on how well they have carried out certain processes and procedures (a reference to perhaps to the inspection regimes mentioned above) rather than what the end result has been for children themselves. The report proposes moving from a system that has become over-bureaucratised and focused on compliance to one that values and develops professional expertise and values the professional judgements of those working with children.

Read *The Munro Review of Child Protection – a child-centred system* (2011c) at www.education. gov.uk/publications/standard/publicationDetail/Page1/CM%208062

REFLECTIVE TASK
What are the main changes In the *Munro Review*? How do you think they will affect your area of work?

Benefits of integrated working

There is general agreement across all those involved in delivering services for children that professionals working together across disciplinary boundaries provide a more co-ordinated and supportive service for children and their carers. Some of the benefits include:

- Earlier, holistic identification of needs – Being able to identify more completely, accurately and speedily the additional needs of children and young people is the critical first step towards meeting those needs at an early stage and preventing problems escalating.
- Earlier, more co-ordinated and effective intervention – Intervening early and in a manner that maximises the available resources (for example, by avoiding duplication of activities, by building on earlier interventions, by working together as a team) secures better outcomes for children. Effective integrated practice is already in place in many areas, for example SureStart, Youth Offending Teams and Drug Action Teams.
- Improved information-sharing across agencies – Being able to identify other practitioners working with a child or young person and sharing information legally and professionally is vital for early and effective intervention and for safeguarding. Improved practice in information sharing will lead to:
  - more holistic assessment of needs;
  - less duplication of effort;
  - improved understanding of service delivery options;
  - better quality and more appropriate referrals.
- Better service experience for children and families – Integrated working will deliver a better service experience that is less stressful to children, young people and families through providing:
  - a child and family-centred approach;
  - improved access to information, advice and support;
  - fewer assessments and less repetition;
  - easier, less bureaucratic access to a range of services;

- faster access to targeted services and with less stigma as a result of closer links between these targeted services and universal services.
- Benefits to practitioners and organisations – In addition, there are also significant benefits for practitioners and organisations in:
  - increased confidence in making decisions about sharing information – due to clearer cross-government guidance;
  - less time spent on administrative processes – due to improved access to information on services and practitioners working with children;
  - improved access to services through reduced bureaucracy;
- Improved quality referrals received – more accurately targeted and more evidence-basedi mproved quality referrals received – more accurately targeted and more evidence-based.

(adapted from DCSF, 2007)

Challenges of integrated working

However, there are obvious challenges to working in an integrated way with other professionals and some of these include the following.

- Communication barriers – All professionals have their own language for talking about their work, often referred to as 'jargon'. If others working in the same area are unaware of this jargon, it can present a real barrier to understanding and may in some cases result in real misrepresentation of the facts.
- Geographical barriers – Where a service is located may act as a barrier to working with other services in terms of being able to meet easily to discuss issues. The advent of communication technology such as tele-conferencing may help to alleviate this issue.
- Psychological barriers – The way professionals in different services think about their work with children may also serve as a barrier to working collaboratively. For example, a teacher may be fully focused on ensuring a pupil attends school to keep up with their GCSE work, whereas the social worker may feel that attendance at family meetings during school time is paramount in terms of looking at the wider issues affecting the child's situation. Talking and working together in an open and holistic way with other professionals can help to overcome some of these difficulties.
- Competing or conflicting targets – Issues can be caused when practitioners are working to different targets for the multi-agency service and for their home agencies. There is the potential for these targets to be competing or conflicting, leaving the practitioners confused about what they are supposed to do and potentially in danger of failing to meet one or both of the targets.

REFLECTIVE TASK

What other challenges can you think of in terms of working across professional boundaries?

Skills for team working

This section looks at some of the skills you may need to develop for team working.

Developing and enhancing the skills needed to work as an effective member of a team is an important aspect of professional development for support staff working within the wider school workforce. These skills include developing oral and written communication skills, time-management and goal-setting skills, problem-solving and conflict-resolution skills. One of the most important skills for ensuring that you develop a good rapport with colleagues is skilful listening, sometimes referred to as active listening. Characteristics of active listening are:

- establishing a calm atmosphere;
- removing or minimising distractions;
- concentrating on the speaker's verbal and physical cues;
- establishing and maintaining positive eye contact;
- using supportive body language – affirmative noises, gestures, facial expressions;
- hearing the message, not just the words;
- showing patience and empathy;
- being aware of and avoiding personal prejudice.

REFLECTIVE TASK

Bearing in mind the above list, monitor your own listening skills over the next few days, both in work and at home – are you an active listener?

PRACTICAL TASK

To assess your own teamwork skills, take the audit below to find out where you may need to develop using the following ratings.

1 = Strongly disagree
2 = Disagree
3 = Not sure
4 = Agree
5 = Strongly agree

Use the results to consider where your development needs are in terms of team working. You should identify where your teamwork performance is not adequate and aim to improve in these areas. A better measure may be to ask your team colleagues to rate you on these dimensions, so you have more objective feedback.

Communication	1	2	3	4	5
I understand and use communication networks, making sufficient contact with colleagues					
I communicate openly and supportively					
I listen actively and non-evaluatively					
There is a consistency between my verbal and non-verbal behaviour					
I value and offer warm greetings and small talk with colleagues					

Goal setting and performance management	1	2	3	4	5
I help establish clear and challenging team goals					
I monitor and give supportive feedback on team and individual performance					

Planning and co-ordination	1	2	3	4	5
I help to co-ordinate activities, information and working together between members					
I help to clarify tasks and roles of team members and ensure balance of workloads					
I respond positively and flexibly to feedback from team members					

Collaborative problem solving	1	2	3	4	5
I identify problems requiring participation of all team members in decision making					
I use appropriate ways of involving team members in decision making					
I explore and support proposals for innovation in the team					

Innovation	1	2	3	4	5
I try to introduce improved methods of doing things at work					
I have ideas that significantly improve the way the job is done					
I suggest new working methods to the people I work with					
I contribute to changes in the way my team works					
I am receptive to new ideas that I can use to improve things in my team					

(adapted from West, 2004)

CHAPTER SUMMARY

- Integrated working with professional colleagues from a variety of disciplines and backgrounds is increasingly the norm.
- Integrated inspection/assessment frameworks mean that developing good working relationships across agencies is vital.
- There are benefits and challenges to working in this way and developing the skills and knowledge to be able to work in teams is essential.
- The role of support staff within schools has expanded massively over recent years.

REFERENCES

Department for Children, Schools and Families (DCSF) (2005) *14–19 Education and Skills*. London: DCSF.

Department for Children, Schools and Families (DCSF) (2007) *Integrated Working Training Materials*. London: DCSF.

Department for Children, Schools and Families (DCSF) (2008) *Promoting Achievement, Valuing Success: A strategy for 14–19 qualifications*. London: DCSF.

Department for Education and Skills (DfES) (2002) *Investment for Reform*. London: DfES.

Department for Education and Skills (DfES) (2003a) *Raising Standards and Tackling Workload: A national agreement*. London: DfES.

Department for Education and Skills (DfES) (2003b) *Every Child Matters: Change for children*. Norwich: TSO.

Department for Education and Skills (DfES) (2005a) *The Children's Workforce Strategy*. London: DfES.

Department for Education and Skills (DfES) (2005b) *Extended Schools: Building on experience*. London: DfES.

Department for Education (DfE) (2010) *The Importance of Teaching – The Schools White Paper*. London: DfE.

Department for Education (DfE) (2011a) *Special Educational Needs and Disability*. Green Paper. London: DfE.

Department for Education (DfE) (2011b) *Report on Vocational Education – The Wolf Report*. London: DfE.

Department for Education (DfE) (2011c) *The Munro Review of Child Protection Final Report: A child-centred system*. London: DfE

Laming, L. (2003) *The Victoria Climbié Inquiry*. London: Department of Health.

Office for Standards in Education (Ofsted) (2010) *Workforce reform in schools – has it made a difference?* London: Ofsted.

PricewaterhouseCoopers (PWC) (2001) *Teacher Workload Study: Final Report*. London: DfES.

Stevenson, H. (2007) Restructuring teachers' work and trade union responses in England: bargaining for change? *American Educational Research Journal*, 44(2): 224–51.

Training and Development Agency (TDA) (2007) *Case Study*. Full case study available online at www.tda.gov.uk/school-leader/effective-staff-deployment/effective-deployment-of-school-leaders/case-studies/cherwell.aspx (accessed 1/3/2012).

West, M.A. (2004) *Effective Teamwork: Practical lessons from organisational research* (2nd edition). Oxford: Blackwell.

4 SUPPORTING THE WHOLE CHILD

Maureen Judge and Felix Obadan

CHAPTER OBJECTIVES

By the end of this chapter you will:

- have explored aspects of pastoral support and personal, social and health education (PSHE) and citizenship, including social and emotional aspects of learning (SEAL);
- understand the relationship between these aspects and achievement, and be able to identify some of the main strategies used to address these needs, such as circle time, one-to-one support, mentoring, peer group support systems, playground activities and thematic topics such as anti-bullying weeks;
- be aware of the various roles support staff can play in these respective fields.

LINKS TO **HLTA** STANDARDS

1. Understand the key factors that affect children's and young people's learning and progress.
2. Know how to contribute to effective personalised provision by taking practical account of diversity.
3. Have sufficient understanding of area(s) of expertise to support the development, learning and progress of children and young people.
4. Know how to support learners in accessing the curriculum in accordance with the special educational needs (SEN) code of practice and disabilities legislation.
5. Know how other frameworks, which support the development and well-being of children and young people, impact upon practice.
6. Plan how to support the inclusion of the children and young people in the learning activities.
7. Use effective strategies to promote positive behaviour.
8. Recognise and respond appropriately to situations that challenge equality of opportunity.
9. Organise and manage learning activities in ways that keep learners safe.

It is important to remember that the HLTA standards that address professional attributes link to the objectives in this chapter; however, for further understanding of these, you need to read Chapter 2, which addresses them in depth.

Introduction

This chapter will examine the demands of the Children Act 2004, enshrining the *Every Child Matters Agenda*. It will explore aspects of pastoral support and personal, social and health education (PSHE) and citizenship, including social and emotional aspects of learning (SEAL). It will discuss the relationship of these aspects to achievement and will introduce some of the main strategies used to address these needs: circle time, one-to-one support, mentoring, peer group support systems, playground activities and thematic topics such as anti-bullying weeks. It will address the various roles support staff can play in this field.

Background

The United Nations Convention on the Rights of the Child was ratified by the UK in 1991 (UNICEF/UK, 2011). The rights enshrined in the United Nations Convention on the Rights of the Child covers four main categories. They are:

- *the right to survive*
- *the right to be safe*
- *the right to belong*
- *the right to develop*

(Save the Children, 2006)

The government of the United Kingdom by signing the Convention has the responsibility to ensure that the rights of children are met and respected by all individuals who work with children as well as local authorities responsible for children. The Children Act (2004), which legalised the outcomes of the *Every Child Matters* (ECM) *Agenda* (DfES, 2003), represents a major step forward in putting into practice the rights given in this Convention.

The ECM Agenda (DfES, 2003) proposed changes in policy and legislation in England to maximise opportunities and minimise risks for all children and young people, focusing services more effectively around the needs of children, young people and families (OPSI, 2007). As stated in Chapter 1, the government's aim was:

that every child, whatever their background or their circumstances, will have the support they need to:
- *Be healthy*
- *Stay safe*
- *Enjoy and achieve*
- *Make a positive contribution*
- *Achieve economic well-being.*

(DfES, 2003)

Demands of the *Every Child Matters Agenda*

To fulfil effectively the demands of the five outcomes of ECM, schools faced the challenge of introducing new concepts and ways of working to their structures. Provisions are now made to accommodate activities such as extended schools, personalised learning and healthy schools, as well as expanding the workforce. Coombs and Calvert (2008, p1) suggest that staffing in schools has changed dramatically since the remodelling of the workforce, with *now more Teaching Assistants (TAs) than teachers, not to mention lunchtime supervisors, learning mentors and others in various support roles*. Subsequently, one of the challenges is to ensure that all staff, teaching and non-teaching, are fully aware of the implications of the ECM Agenda (DfES, 2003) and the necessity to identify their training requirements in order to meet the needs of the child (Reid, 2005). Roche and Tucker (2007, p220) argue that the training will need to address the *Common Core of Skills and Knowledge for the Children's Workforce* (DfES, 2005), which has six broad areas of expertise, along with meeting the demands of, for example, becoming an extended school.

Pastoral support

In June 2005, as part of the *Excellence and Enjoyment* strategy, the social and emotional aspects of learning (SEAL) programme was launched (DfES, 2005). The aim of the programme was to provide guidance and curriculum materials for developing children's social, behavioural and emotional skills.

The importance of pastoral support, as documented in the implementation of the Children Act 2004 (OPSI, 2007), reflects a wide range of issues relating to the implementation of the legislation. It also focuses particularly on the challenges faced by schools as they embark upon multi-agency partnerships, and on the ability to develop integrated ways of working with vulnerable children and young people.

Pastoral support systems need to be in place for both pupils and staff. These provide confidential advice and pastoral care, and the provision for these needs affords schools the opportunity to cater for situations such as bereavement and other major life-changing experiences. This helps guard against stigmatisation of and discrimination against such pupils.

Lead professionals have been introduced, such as pastoral staff, who have trusting relationships with the child or parent. These may be in a better position to discuss initial concerns with a child or parent, and work with them over a given period, rather than a social worker with whom the family has had no previous contact. Ongoing curriculum and pastoral support ensures that young people make progress during all learning programmes. Short practical intervention programmes provide support to young persons at risk of disaffection or permanent exclusion. These should be initiated by the school but should be agreed with parents or carers and involve the local authority and other agencies.

Ofsted (2010) maintains that schools that are most successful in preventing exclusion have policies that tackle underlying causes of poor behaviour with strategies such as pastoral support programmes. Young people in public care usually prefer not to be treated differently from others but sensitive support, such as that recommended as part of Pastoral Support Programmes (PSPs) or Individual Education Plans (IEPs), can prevent problems as well as deal with any emerging or existing behavioural problems. Pastoral support can include providing a 'buddy' for a child new to the school or the help of a learning mentor or counsellor. Crow (2008) stresses that, according to the Qualifications and Curriculum Authority (QCA), one of the key ways in which a school can show its contribution to the Every Child Matters outcomes is through a curriculum that supports personal development and the promotion of well-being.

PRACTICAL TASK

Examine your school policy on PSHE and find out how your school curriculum supports personal development and promotes the well-being of pupils.

Social and emotional aspects of learning

Weare (2007) believes that social and emotional learning is absolutely central to the achievement of ECM (2007, p239) and agrees with Crow (2008) in that the main aims of SEAL are to develop skills that encourage children to understand and manage their emotions. The children and young people then need to apply these new skills when interacting and building relationships with others. In addition, Crow (2008) draws our attention to the challenges and demands of implementing SEAL, one being the curriculum congestion and:

> lack of an underlying or clearly unifying rationale for PSHE or SEAL, both of which are perceived as tapping into broadly the same vein – something about 'emotions' but not subject learning.
>
> (Crow, 2008, p48)

Another possible challenge might be teachers' lack of confidence in delivering this aspect of the curriculum.

SEAL is described by Crow (2008) as a whole-school approach with a curriculum focus, which can be clearly seen in the Morrison and Matthews (2006) research 'How pupils can be helped to develop socially and emotionally in science lessons'. Their belief is that, if teachers incorporated elements of pastoral work into their teaching through collaborative group work, it would reduce the conflict in class rather than keeping it as a separate issue normally addressed by the form tutor.

The researchers draw our attention to work by Megahy (cited in Morrison and Matthews, 2006), who states that attention to pastoral care can improve achievement. Arguably, the results from their research clearly show this to be true. The research consisted of classes where groups made up of two boys and two girls were encouraged to work together and discuss their work.

The class teachers who took part in the research gave very positive comments on how the pupils' behaviour had improved, with less conflict, especially between the boys, who were even willing to engage with their emotions (Morrison and Matthews, 2006, p15). Pupils were more disposed to work collaboratively in mixed-gender groups and contribute to the lesson without fear of ridicule by their peers. The difference in the research classes and the control class was that the control class had not developed support systems. An interesting observation by the class teachers was that, even after the research had finished, pupils who joined the research groups appeared subconsciously to recognise the social and emotional behaviour of the other pupils and to conform.

Greenhalgh (1994) supports this view, highlighting that emotional development is a key aspect in enabling pupils to learn, and that pupils can become more effective learners when they develop emotionally. Steiner (cited in Morrison and Matthews, 2006) defined emotional literacy as:

> *the ability to understand your emotions, the ability to listen to others and empathise with their emotions, and the ability to express emotions productively.*

> *Emotional literacy improves relationships . . . [and] . . . makes co-operative work possible.*
> (Morrison and Matthews, 2006, p11)

There are many definitions of emotional literacy, however; the definition by the organisation Antidote (2003) states that *Emotional Literacy is the practice of thinking individually and collectively about how emotions shape our actions, and of using emotional understanding to enrich our thinking* (cited in Morrison and Matthews, 2006, p11).

This view suggests that, if children have a better understanding of their emotions, their behaviour will improve and this will also impact on their learning. Furthermore, Radcliffe agrees by highlighting the importance of developing emotional literacy in *helping children make the link between emotional feelings, thinking and behaviour* (2008, p1). Consequently, the teacher has an important role to play in promoting this aptitude and will benefit directly from its application in his or her classroom.

Additionally, Radcliffe (2008) suggests that a good way to implement SEAL across the whole school is through assemblies. This addresses the need for whole-school ownership of the underpinning values espoused by the programme.

REFLECTIVE TASK

How might emotional literacy improve behaviour and combat bullying in schools?

Bullying

Bullying is a form of poor behaviour that causes particular unhappiness and disruption to the learning of individual pupils. Anyone can experience bullying, but there is evidence that some groups, including disabled children and looked-after children, are more likely to be bullied than others.

Schools should have a policy to prevent bullying among pupils and must make sure that it is in line with the Human Rights Act 1998 (DfE, 2011). Anti-bullying policies should:

- identify the extent and nature of bullying that takes place in schools;
- raise the profile of bullying and its effects on children and young people's emotional health and well-being, life chances and achievement;
- establish a culture where bullying is not acceptable, through the promotion of policies and practices that prevent or reduce opportunities for bullying to occur, and deal swiftly, fairly and sensitively when they do;
- involve parents, carers, children and young people in developing and implementing anti-bullying strategies;

- embody equality of opportunity, celebrate diversity and be responsive to individual needs and differences.

This policy also needs to recognise the particular vulnerability of looked-after children. It should be monitored by the governing body of the school as it shows how concerned they are about pupils' health and safety (DfE, 2011). The governing body should ensure that the school's anti-bullying and behaviour policies are flexible in their understanding of care issues and support early intervention (DfE, 2011). The school must inform pupils, in particular looked-after children, so that they understand the process for making complaints (DfE, 2011).

PRACTICAL TASK

Locate and read your school anti-bullying policy to see if the above points are included within the policy. Does the policy need updating? Do you know what the procedure is if a child informs you that they are being bullied?

REFLECTIVE TASK

What could be done to ensure that pupils are not too frightened to speak out and ask for help?

Mellor and Munn (2000) suggest that circle time can have a major impact on young people by promoting respect for others and therefore has a significant role in the prevention of bullying.

What is circle time?

Although circle time has been practised in many primary schools since Jenny Mosley first introduced it in the 1990s, it is only recently that secondary schools are recognising the benefits. Circle time is designed to address behavioural, social and emotional problems for children in a safe and secure environment.

The circle time model is a whole-school approach and, therefore, all staff need to be involved in order to maintain a positive school management system to:

- *promote positive behaviour;*
- *create a caring and respectful school ethos;*
- *help children develop their self-esteem and self-confidence;*
- *provide efficient and effective systems and support for staff;*
- *create great lunchtimes and playtimes;*
- *nurture the creativity in all people in school.*

(Mosley, 2008, p1)

It can be seen from the above that circle time will help schools to address all five outcomes from the Children Act 2004. The sessions can be linked to PSHE and citizenship. Circle time involves weekly sessions of approximately half an hour with the teacher or TA sitting in a circle with the pupils and includes activities, games and the practice of speaking and listening skills, often in a round. The key elements are:

- *improving the morale and self-esteem of staff;*
- *listening systems for children and adults;*
- *the Golden Rules: a system of behavioural rules for children;*
- *incentives: a weekly celebration to congratulate the children for keeping the Golden Rules;*
- *sanctions: the partial withdrawal of the Golden Time incentive;*
- *[a] lunchtime policy.*

(Mosley, 2008, p1)

Many TAs are either included in quality circle time or run the session themselves; therefore, the need for consistency is very important. Circle time has clear set ground rules that must be adhered to if it is going to be successful, with children understanding the consequences if the rules are broken.

REFLECTIVE TASK

Does your school use circle time as a whole-school approach? If so, list the benefits for the pupil, the class teacher and the school.

CASE STUDY 1

Sarah, a TA employed in a primary school, was working very closely with a Year 1 child named Mary, who was very quiet, had low self-esteem and was reluctant to speak to any adults or even her peers. The lunchtime supervisor had also noticed her reluctance to join in any activities and saw her very often walking around the playground on her own. The class teacher was finding it very difficult to assess Mary's level of attainment fully and was very concerned about her social and emotional development. Sarah was asked to work with the pupil to encourage her to communicate and join in lunchtime activities.

REFLECTIVE TASK

How would you work with this pupil to help her overcome her difficulties? Make a list of the strategies you would employ and the activities you might include. Now read the TA response.

TA response

I observed Mary by sitting with the group that she was working in. She appeared to be coping well with the work set by the class teacher and on occasion spoke very quietly to one particular pupil, Clare, if she was stuck. This was reassuring and I immediately decided to try to develop this communication into a friendship that would hopefully develop her confidence, social skills and self-esteem. I organised the pupils into pairs to work on number and phonic activities, and encouraged them to explain their strategies and results. At first, Mary was very reluctant to speak when she thought anyone other than Clare was listening. I had a great deal of information on circle time and its benefits in developing pupils' social and emotional skills, so I approached the class teacher and suggested that she try this with Mary's group before introducing it to the whole class. The class teacher agreed, so I found a quiet area, sat with the pupils and explained the rules of circle time, and that they should only speak when it was their turn and they were holding the teddy bear. I assured Mary that she only needed to talk if she wanted to and, if she didn't, she just needed to say 'pass'. I introduced an activity called 'Rounds' because the learning aims were:

- *to share feelings;*
- *to evaluate experience;*
- *to develop talking and listening.*

I felt that this activity would not only address Mary's needs but would also develop the social and emotional skills of the other members of the group. The activity involved the pupils finishing the sentence 'I feel happy when . . .' to encourage them to share their feelings. I decided to focus on a happy occasion first to gain their confidence and ensure that they enjoyed the activity. As expected, Mary didn't speak on the first round, so I tried again and asked the pupils to think of another time when they felt happy. The other pupils asked Mary to join in and share her 'happy times', as one pupil put it. At first, she struggled getting the words out but it was a start. The group continued to have circle time once a week and, after six weeks, Mary was starting to open up and talk to the group. The class teacher had noticed her increased confidence in class when she was working with the group, so decided to continue with circle time and was keen to introduce it to the whole class, and Mary coped well. The friendship developed between Mary and Clare, extending to after school. Mary is still quiet but has much more confidence in class, contributing to discussion and joining in activities in the playground. The lunchtime supervisor says that Mary is a happy little girl now and it's good to see her joining in and having fun.

REFLECTIVE TASK

Compare your ideas/strategies with the TA in case study 1. Were any of your strategies and activities the same? Would you have used a different approach and, if so, why?

One-to-one support

There are many reasons why a child might be given one-to-one support, ranging from medical to behavioural or individual learning needs. Each case is assessed on its own merits and the provision that is put in place depends on the severity of assistance the child needs. This can be provided by the local authority, if the child has a statement of SEN, or the school, depending on the reason for the support. The support staff who work with these children play a very special role in helping them overcome barriers to their learning, develop their self-esteem and raise their academic achievement.

PRACTICAL TASK

Consider the ways in which a learning support assistant (LSA), special support assistant (SSA) or TA can provide direct one-to-one pupil support. Use the diagram opposite to list the tasks they might perform.

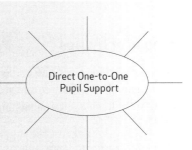

Direct One-to-One Pupil Support

CASE STUDY 2

Stephen is 12 years old and has moderate learning difficulties and behavioural problems. He achieved below average marks in Year 6 National Tests and has, therefore, been granted one-to-one support in secondary school for core subjects. The aim of the LSA is to monitor Stephen's behaviour in lessons and develop strategies to keep him focused and on task. He is very disruptive and argumentative towards his peers and disrespectful to his class teachers. Consequently, he is often removed from class, put on a report card and given detention.

REFLECTIVE TASK

If you were the LSA assigned to Stephen, what strategies would you employ to improve his behaviour and encourage him to work co-operatively in lessons?

Learning support assistant response

When meeting Stephen for the first time, he wouldn't speak to me and when he eventually did he was argumentative and aggressive. However, I explained that I'd be supporting him in particular lessons and my aim was to help him remain in class and stay focused on his lessons, which would stop him getting detention and being on a report card. I found that, in lessons, Stephen didn't always follow the teacher's instructions, simply because he didn't understand. He became very frustrated with himself and this manifested itself in very poor behaviour. Subsequently, I set down some ground rules with Stephen in line with the school's behaviour policy, and told him that I could help explain the teacher's instructions if he didn't understand them. I was able to explain what the teacher wanted in a way that Stephen could understand and also break the work down into manageable steps, helping him to achieve and building his self-esteem. If Stephen's concentration lapsed, I either spoke his name or asked him a question to help him refocus, which allowed him to complete work and even answer questions. Once Stephen's self-esteem improved, his behaviour began to improve also, but I realised it would take quite a while to gain Stephen's trust completely. I hope to instil in Stephen the need to take responsibility for his actions and the need to talk about his feelings, rather than just reacting with hostility in certain situations. I'm happy with the progress Stephen is making but we still have a long way to go.

PRACTICAL TASK

The LSA is making links to citizenship, in which the child needs to take responsibility for their own behaviour. Locate the school PSHE and citizenship policy and identify other strategies that can be used to help children like Stephen. Then reflect on what, if anything, you would do differently.

Playground activities

Children spend around 25 per cent of their school day in the playground. This can be very daunting for a number of children and young people who are excluded from activities that, in many cases, are dominated by a small number of children who decide who can be 'included'.

PRACTICAL TASK

Make a list of all the playground activities that you or the lunchtime supervisor organise and do with the children.

The government and the Youth Sport Trust have been working together since 2001 on a three-phase project called 'Zoneparc' to try to overcome the problem and ensure that playgrounds are active, exhilarating, safe and secure places for all (Youth Sports Trust, 2008). Zoneparc is just one of the projects that the Youth Sport Trust is promoting that address the five outcomes of the *ECM Agenda* (DfES, 2003). It is a primary playground project aimed at making playtimes safer and children more active, while tackling social exclusion and improving behaviour.

One of the approaches they promote is the division of play space into areas for different activities, for example a quiet play area for reading and talking, a sports area, preferably fenced for fast-flowing mini-sports or ball games, and a general play area, possibly incorporating a 'stage' for pupil-led performances of dance and theatre. Many primary school playgrounds now incorporate this type of zoning. Supervision can be an issue, with few lunchtime assistants available; however, if the dynamic and extremely physical activities are organised and supervised separately, it is probable that the other areas will have many fewer incidents requiring intervention.

What is important here is for schools to acknowledge the significance of playtime as a means of developing the whole child, rather than leaving it as a 'non-learning' time that frequently may be boring and, at times, actively harmful to the pupils. This type of activity can improve pupils' well-being by building their self-esteem and influencing or even changing their attitudes to learning, breaking down barriers and providing them with a brighter future. It reduces lunch- and playtime trouble too, and that is something of benefit to all school staff.

REFLECTIVE TASK

In what ways do your school lunchtime organisation or supervision promote positive behaviour, healthy lifestyles and personal and social learning?

Many lunchtime supervisors are also TAs and are in a very privileged position to help identify the early signs of problems that children may be experiencing. They also have the opportunity to influence the children's future and help and guide them in becoming model citizens, taking responsibility for their own actions. They are a key part of the school staff and need to be acknowledged and valued as such.

CHAPTER SUMMARY

- There are demands and challenges inherent in meeting the UN Convention of the Rights of the Child for schools that are introducing new initiatives to address the five outcomes of the Children Act 2004.
- The role of support staff is continually changing and there is a need to keep up to date with new initiatives and legislation.
- All staff, teaching or non-teaching, can make a difference and have an impact on a child's life and future.

REFERENCES

Coombs, S. and Calvert, M. (2008) *Every Child Matters: Challenges and opportunities for CPD*. Available online at www.teachingexpertise.com/topic/every-child-matters (accessed 2/3/12).

Crow, F. (2008) Learning for well being: personal, social and health education and a changing curriculum. *Pastoral Care in Education*, 26(1): 43–51.

Department for Education (DfE) (2011) *Preventing and Tackling Bullying*, DfE-00062–2011, London: DfE. Available online at www.education.gov.uk/publications/standard/publicationDetail/Page1/DFE-00062–2011 (accessed 2/3/12).

Department for Education and Skills (DfES) (2003) *Every Child Matters*. Available online at www.education.gov.uk/consultations/downloadableDocs/EveryChildMatters.pdf (accessed 2/3/12).

Department for Education and Skills (DfES) (2005) *Common Core of Skills and Knowledge for the Children's Workforce*. London: DfES.

Greenhalgh, P. (1994) *Emotional Growth and Learning*. London: Routledge.

Mellor, A. and Munn, P. (2000) *Information on Circle Time*. Available online at www.anti bullying.net/circletimesheet3.htm (accessed 1/3/12).

Morrison, L. and Matthews, B. (2006) How pupils can be helped to develop socially and emotionally in science lessons. *Pastoral Care*, 24(1): 10–19.

Mosley, J. (2008) What is Quality Circle Time? Available online at www.circle-time.co.uk/site/what_is_quality_circle_time (accessed 1/3/12).

Office of Public Sector Information (OPSI) (2007) Explanatory Notes to the Children Act 2004. Available online at www.opsi.gov.uk/acts/acts2004/en/ukpgaen_20040031_en.pdf (accessed 17/2/12).

Ofsted (2010) Personal, social, health and economic education in schools. Report ref 090222. Available online at www.ofsted.gov.uk/resources/personal-social-health-and-economic-education (accessed 30/11/11).

Radcliffe, B. (2008) Secondary Assemblies for SEAL. Available online at www.teachingexpertise.com/e-bulletins/secondary-assembly-forth-bridge-doing-job-properly-5409 (accessed 2/3/12).

Reid, K. (2005) The implications of Every Child Matters and the Children Act for schools. *Pastoral Care*, 23(1): 12–18.

Roche, J. and Tucker, S. (2007) Every Child Matters: 'tinkering' or 'reforming' – an analysis of the development of the Children Act (2004) from an educational perspective. *Education 3–13*, 35(3): 213–23.

Save the Children (2006) *Children's Rights: A teacher's guide*. London: Save the Children. Available online at www.savethechildren.org.uk/en/docs/childrensrights_teachersguide.pdf (accessed 30/11/11).

UNICEF/UK (2011) *The UN Convention*. Available online at www.unicef.org.uk/UNICEFs-Work/Our-mission (accessed 30/11/11).

Weare, K. (2007) Delivering Every Child Matters: the central role of social and emotional learning in schools. *Education*, 3–13, 35(3): 239–48.

Youth Sports Trust (2008) Zoneparc. Available online at www.youthsporttrust.org/; www.primarytimes.net/teacher_times_news_youth_sports_trust.php (accessed 1/3/2012).

FURTHER READING

Lorenz, S. (2002) *Effective In-class Support*. London: David Fulton Publishers.

5 INCLUSION and SEN

Linda Dunne and Lisa O'Connor

CHAPTER OBJECTIVES

By the end of this chapter you will:

- have gained an understanding of the development of inclusive education;
- be more critically aware of the concept and nature of inclusion;
- have reflected upon how you can enhance inclusive practice and contribute to an inclusive ethos and culture;
- be able to identify good practice in the support of pupils with SEN.

LINKS TO **HLTA** STANDARDS

1. Understand the key factors that affect children and young people's learning and progress.
2. Know how to contribute to effective personalised provision by taking practical account of diversity.
3. Know how to support learners in accessing the curriculum in accordance with the special educational needs (SEN) code of practice and disabilities legislation.
4. Plan how they will support the inclusion of the children and young people in the learning activities.
5. Recognise and respond appropriately to situations that challenge equality of opportunity.
6. Organise and manage learning activities in ways which keep learners safe.

Introduction

The role of Teaching Assistants (TAs) in supporting teaching and learning, and the way in which that support is provided, have been seen to be crucial to the inclusion process in schools (Sorsby, 2004; Richards and Armstrong, 2008). This chapter considers the concept and practice of inclusion in relation to special educational needs. It will encourage you to reflect upon inclusion, on what it might mean and on how you can enhance the inclusive practice and culture of your workplace.

Inclusive school reform

Inclusion may be seen as a concept, or an idea, that suggests that nobody is excluded. It seems to be something that has 'always been there' and it has become part of taken-for-granted everyday practices in schools. However, inclusive school reform has a history that has shaped where we are today.

Inclusion necessitates change to the fabric and culture of schooling both nationally and internationally (UNESCO, 1994). Inclusion in the UK has been accompanied by an increase in the number of TAs working in schools to assist teaching and learning and to meet learning needs. The timeline below shows policies, initiatives and legislation that have called for increased inclusion.

In acknowledging inclusion, a school's curriculum needs to be accessible for all children. Planning for inclusion draws on a range of access strategies, varied teaching styles and appropriate, realistic learning objectives.

A timeline of significant legislation and initiatives relating to inclusion in education

1978	Warnock Report. Introduced term 'special educational needs' (SEN) and a 'continuum' of need.
1981	Education Act. Definitions of SEN.
1988	Education Reform Act. Right of all children to access a broad and balanced curriculum.
1994	Salamanca Statement. International moves towards inclusion based on rights and entitlement for all children (UNESCO).
1994	*Code of Practice on the Identification and Assessment of Pupils with SEN.* A five-stage guidance model for schools.
1995	Disability Discrimination Act.
1996	Education Act. Strengthened children's rights to be educated in mainstream schools.
1997	*Excellence for All Children: Meeting SEN.* Introduced term 'inclusion'.
1998	*Meeting SEN: A programme of action.* Aimed at developing more inclusive approaches.
2000	Revised National Curriculum. Formulated upon three core inclusion-oriented principles: setting suitable learning challenges, responding to pupils' diverse needs and overcoming potential barriers to learning and assessment for individuals and groups of children.
2000	*Index for Inclusion.* Inclusive indicators and support for schools in developing inclusion.
2001	Revised Code of Practice.
2001	Special Educational Needs and Disability Act.
2001	*Inclusive Schooling.* Guidelines for developing effective inclusion.
2003	*Every Child Matters: Change for children.* Sets out the future direction of services working around children.
2004	The Children Act. Provides the legislative spine of Every Child Matters.
2004	*Removing Barriers to Achievement.* Government strategy for SEN and inclusion.
2005	Leading on Inclusion
2007	*Inclusion Development Programme.* Early intervention and strategic approaches.
2009	Rose Review of the Primary Curriculum
2009	*Lamb Inquiry Special Educational Needs and Parental Confidence*
2011	*Support and aspiration: A new approach to special educational needs and disability*
2011	Education Act

Inclusion is an unending process that involves change and improvement. Some of the more general aims behind inclusive education policy initiatives and developments have been to:

- improve the outcomes for all pupils and to narrow the gaps between the lowest and highest achievers;
- promote early recognition and intervention;
- increase the confidence of all practitioners (teachers and TAs);
- work in partnership with parents and agencies
- support schools and settings to be more effective at strategic approaches to support and intervention.

PRACTICAL TASK

Your school may have its own policy that relates to inclusion. Find out about your school's policy or policies that pertain to inclusion, aspects of inclusion or equality of opportunity.

REFLECTIVE TASK

Reflect upon your understanding of the term inclusion. What principles do you associate with inclusion and how do they underpin your approach to working with children?

What is inclusion?

Despite its infusion in policy and references to participation, access, meeting diverse needs and so on, there is no single shared definition of inclusion and it is wide open to different meanings and interpretations. Some researchers and organisational bodies do offer definitions of what inclusion is or what it ought to be. For example, Ofsted, the school inspectorate, quite a long time ago, offered this definition:

Educational inclusion . . . is about equal opportunities for all pupils . . . it pays particular attention to the provision for, and achievement of, different groups of pupils.

(Ofsted, 2001)

Groups identified for inclusion include gender, black and minority ethnic and faith groups; travellers; and learners with special educational needs (SEN). Integration and inclusion are very different and thinking about inclusion solely in terms of school placement or where a child is educated would be mistaken. Likewise, thinking about inclusion solely in terms of SEN would be misguided. Inclusion is about the rights of all children and it pays attention to how the attitudes and practices of schooling can sometimes marginalise or exclude children because of their ethnicity, race, gender, ability or other factors.

The Centre for Studies on Inclusive Education (www.csie.org.uk) emphasises that inclusion is about rights, equity issues and social justice. It defines inclusion as:

Involving the processes of increasing the participation of students in, and reducing their exclusion from the cultures, curricula and communities of local schools.

Inclusion is about creating a secure, accepting, collaborating and stimulating school in which everyone is valued and can do their best. In an inclusive school, the inclusive ethos permeates all school policies so that learning and participation are increased for all children, and school practices reflect the inclusive ethos and policies of the school (Booth et al., 2002).

Ethos and culture

There appears to be general agreement that inclusion is related to the ethos and culture of a school and this is based on values and how people relate to, and treat, each other. Questions of school ethos, culture and belonging help us to expand the concept of inclusion and to consider diversity more broadly. Every member of school staff, through their practice, can promote and reflect the inclusive culture and policy of the school.

As a TA, you have a responsibility and a vital role to play in promoting and supporting an inclusive 'feeling', ethos and culture. How you relate to children, in terms of teaching and learning, is crucial. Your choice of language, tone of voice and manner, for example, play a large part in establishing an ethos in which children feel safe to make mistakes and take risks with their learning. You can help to create an ethos where children feel respected and valued and where it is acceptable for children to say 'I'll try but I need some help', rather than 'I cannot do it.'

In an inclusive classroom, 'wrong' answers are not dismissed but are seen as interesting, providing an opportunity to explore the thinking that led to the answer, rather than a sign of failure. When a child gives a wrong answer, you might ask for opinions: 'That's interesting – does anyone think differently? Why?' Or you may recognise any part of the child's answer that is correct, then prompt or scaffold the same pupil to answer again rather than going on to other pupils for the 'right' answer. An inclusive teacher or TA will let children know that, if they don't understand, that means that the adult needs to find another way of explaining; it is the adult's problem and not the child's.

> **PRACTICAL TASK**
>
> Locate your school's mission statement or statement that captures its ethos and culture.

> **REFLECTIVE TASK**
>
> Think about the ethos and culture of your school or workplace.
>
> - In what ways is it inclusive?
> - How do you contribute towards your school's ethos?
> - What can you do to help make it more inclusive?

Social/medical models of disability and special educational needs

A helpful framework for approaching understandings of inclusion is provided by the social and medical models of disability. Children with learning difficulties and disabilities used to be, and still are, categorised by a deficit model in that they were 'identified' as having problems or difficulty (deficit) and were subject to 'special' forms of provision. Thinking in terms of 'within-child' deficit, or lack, and categorising children in medical ways, is sometimes referred to as the medical model of disability. This model 'medicalises', or can make a problem out of what are sometimes just differences in natural human attributes or ways of being. Medical models or approaches can be subtle and wide ranging. For example, we inadvertently medicalise dyslexia by talking in terms of 'conditions' and 'diagnosis', and this is not particularly helpful to either the child with the learning needs or to the wider process of inclusion.

Medical models of thinking and of practice were very prevalent prior to moves towards greater inclusion. It is now recognised that it is more appropriate, respectful and more socially just to speak in terms of 'needs', rather than of 'difficulty' or 'conditions'. A social, rather than a medical model of disability looks to the social environment and physical spaces that can exclude or disable people; it looks to attitudes and to changing ways of thinking about, and engaging with, difference. It considers removing barriers to participation in learning.

REFLECTIVE TASK

Think about the language that you use when talking about or working with children whom you support.

- How helpful is it to talk in terms of, for example, 'children with SEN' or 'the SEN child'?
- What effect might this type of language and way of thinking have on a child's identity or sense of self?

What does this mean for a Teaching Assistant?

With regard to supporting teaching and learning, a social model of disability helps us to focus upon a child's needs (rather than their 'difficulties') and on adjusting features of the physical and social environment, curriculum and approaches to teaching and learning to enable those needs to be met. It means that we operate a 'can-do' philosophy and highlight children's strengths and achievements, rather than perceived limitations. Thinking about potential barriers to learning is useful as it helps us to move beyond within-child factors to consider other factors, such as the curriculum, attitudes, ethos and culture of schooling.

Some of the barriers to successful inclusion may be difficult to pin down, but they may include, for example, attitudes towards difference (Thomas and Loxley, 2001) and ways of thinking and speaking that can inadvertently cause harm, discriminate and exclude. Some particular features of schooling may also be a barrier to inclusion. For example, the way that children are grouped and how space is used in schools may have a detrimental effect on learning and participation.

The way that you think about learners' needs and the way that you provide support for children can be crucial to successful inclusion. In the classroom, you need to get your level of support just right, so that you can facilitate engagement, independent learning and participation.

REFLECTIVE TASK

Think about potential barriers to learning and participation in your school. How might they be addressed?

Identifying potential barriers to learning

Inclusion requires that those who work with children are able to understand, and meet, their social, emotional and learning needs. The UK coalition government's consultation *Support and Aspiration* (DES, 2011) states that within schools, support staff can make a real difference to the achievement of pupils with SEN, but they need to be deployed effectively in order to do so. Professional development courses can be helpful in gaining understanding of particular areas of need and of support strategies or interventions that can facilitate inclusion but we need to be cautious about becoming 'experts' or 'specialists' in 'special educational needs' as these terms and ways of thinking (e.g. the expert knows best) can also disable a child and work against inclusion.

In light of the social model of disability, a fundamental question that we might address is: how can we develop knowledge and understanding of particular learning needs without disabling children with that knowledge? There is no easy or straightforward answer to this question, but let us look at barriers to learning and demonstrate how approaches and understandings of these barriers can enable or disable learners. Consider these case studies.

CASE STUDY 1

Paul has been placed on School Action Plus and has input from outside agencies to support his learning. He is a Year 5 child experiencing difficulties in several areas including literacy and has a reading age of 6.2 years. He has undertaken interventions which are implemented in school and the expectation is that they will also be modelled and delivered at home. The school believe that this is good collaborative practice but are concerned that his parents are not becoming as involved as his mum stated they would at the last review meeting.

The teacher expects the TA to support Paul's group in their learning. She does not include the TA in planning and preparation for the lesson and very rarely asks for an evaluation of the activity he has completed. Paul's parents have expressed concerns that they do not fully understand the language used at meetings where a variety of professionals are in attendance. Paul's mum did not have a good experience at school and has recently engaged in parenting classes, where it has been discovered that she cannot read and struggles with understanding the concepts surrounding Paul's learning difficulties.

REFLECTIVE TASK

Looking at case study 1, identify the internal and external barriers to learning and consider how the external barriers are impacting on the learners' needs. Can the internal, or school, barriers alone be addressed?

CASE STUDY 2

Peter works in a secondary school and is employed as an in-class-support TA supporting a small group of Year 8 pupils deemed to have particular learning needs. He is managed by the school special educational needs coordinator (SENCO). As he follows the group around he encounters very different styles of teaching and communication from staff. He supports in a literacy group and works alongside a teacher who often asks for his input into planning and delivery styles for his group, and will ask for an evaluation at the end of each week to plan next steps for the learners. Paul supports in a science lesson and has very little communication with the teacher; he is often given an activity without any real direction or consideration of his own and the learners' knowledge and is rarely asked for feedback concerning the group of learners.

REFLECTIVE TASK

How do relationships between these adults impact on the support for the learner?

Difficulty or difference?

When viewing aspects of learning as a difficulty we should consider that it can just as easily be seen as a learning difference. If it is the school policy to view this as a learning difficulty or deficit, essentially because there is something 'wrong' with the child, then practice will tend to focus on special educational needs, remediation and teaching that is often carried out, as something 'special' that is out of context. However, if it is the policy to view this as a learning difference, one that conveys a range of strengths and weaknesses in common with all learning styles and preferences, then practice is able to focus on inclusion, differentiation and learning.

Viewing learning as a 'difficulty' implies that something is 'wrong' with the learner. This is reminiscent of medical models of need. It leads to a focus on identifying weaknesses rather than celebrating strengths. This, in turn, can result in an emphasis on remediation by specialists, or by 'experts', rather than resolution by knowledgeable class and subject teachers and TAs.

Your skill as a TA lies in achieving a balance between empowerment and challenge. Therefore, viewing any learning need as a difficulty may be to misunderstand the situation. In the mainstream classroom setting, the class teacher and the TA, guided by school ethos, policy and practice, have the power to make these needs a learning difficulty or a learning difference. Some examples of strategies for assisting children with learning needs are listed below. These strategies may, of course, be of benefit to all children.

- Multi-sensory approaches. Multi-sensory teaching means using a range of ways to present information and support independent learning.
- Plan for alternatives to written recording – for example matching, sequencing, sorting, highlighting.
- ICT and the use of software.
- Calculators.
- Number lines, table squares.
- Writing mat templates.
- Timetable icons.
- Instructions posters.
- A 'buddy' (or TA) who can act as a scribe.
- Pair or small group work.

- Dictionaries and thesaurus.
- Word lists.
- Key / common words.

Collaboration and teamwork

When considering barriers to learning and how we address these both inside and outside of the classroom we need to consider just how collaborative our practice really is. When we refer to case study 1 it is highlighted that although we often assume collaboration in a prominent feature of our own setting the reality is that we often need to develop stronger relationships, not only with learners and parents, but also with outside agencies.

The Lamb Inquiry (2009) considers the importance of collaboration and identified four key areas to bring about significant and fundamental changes.

- Communication and engagement with parents rather than standard information.
- A reduction in the specific 'SEN' requirements in favour of covering SEN and Disability in information for all children.
- An increased focus on outcomes for disabled pupils and pupils labelled as SEN.
- Tighter quality assurance and accountability for meeting streamlined requirements.

In relation to this, the need to strengthen communication and engagement with parents obviously becomes the role of those involved in supporting the learner. It is often the case that parents form stronger relationships with TAs, as they are aware of the support they give to the child on a daily basis. Through these relationships schools could create a role of Key Worker so that the parent has a constant contact within the school which could help in engaging them in supporting their child's learning. The Key Worker could also be instrumental in linking parents with support agencies and advising them on the best support for their child's learning. TAs need to be included in multi-agency meetings when all professionals supporting the learner are present, as they undoubtedly often have the most input in the support and will have knowledge of how the child is progressing and if interventions are in fact enabling them to make progress.

> **REFLECTIVE TASK**
> When looking at the range of professionals supporting the learner, consider how much power and impact you feel you have within both the learning environment and multi-agency/review meetings focusing on the learner. Consider all those involved with the learner. Who has the greatest power and impact on the learner and why?

PRACTICAL TASK

Take a look at this checklist for inclusive teaching, adapted from the Inclusive Teaching Observation Checklist for teachers (DfES, 2006), and next time you are supporting teaching and learning, refer to the inclusive indicators. The first box has been done for you.

Inclusive indicator	Evidence
Am I clear about what the individual or group is to learn?	Lesson notes or lesson plan.
Have I identified appropriate learning objectives?	
Is there use of multi-sensory approaches (visual, verbal, kinaesthetic)?	
Is there use of interactive strategies, e.g. pupils having cards to hold up or their own whiteboards?	
Is there use of visual and tangible aids, e.g. real objects, signs or symbols, photographs, computer animations?	
Do I find ways of making abstract concepts concrete, e.g. word problems in mathematics turned into pictures or acted out or modelled with resources?	
Are tasks made more open or more closed according to pupils' needs?	
Over time, do I employ a variety of pupil groupings so that pupils are able to draw on each other's strengths and skills?	
Can all pupils see and hear me, and any resources in use (e.g. background noise avoided where possible, light source in front of me and not behind, pupils' seating carefully planned)?	
Is new or difficult vocabulary clarified, written up, displayed, returned to?	
Do I check for understanding of instructions, e.g. by asking a pupil to explain them in their own words?	
Are questions pitched so as to challenge pupils?	
Is the contribution of all learners valued – is this a secure and supportive learning environment where there is safety to have a go and make mistakes?	
Do I give time and support before responses are required, e.g. personal thinking time, partner talk, persisting with progressively more scaffolding until a pupil can answer?	

Inclusive indicator	Evidence
Do I promote independence, protect self-esteem and increase pupils' inclusion within their peer group?	
Are tasks clearly explained or modelled – checks for understanding, task cards or boards as reminders, time available and expected outcomes made clear?	
Are pupils provided with, and regularly reminded of, resources to help them be independent?	
Is scaffolding used (e.g. problem-solving grids, talk and writing frames, clue cards) to support learners?	
Have I made arrangements where necessary to ensure that all children can access written text or instructions?	
Have I planned alternatives to paper-and-pencil tasks, where appropriate?	
Does the teacher make effective use of ICT as an access strategy?(e.g. speech-supported or sign-supported software, on-screen word banks, predictive word processing)	
Is appropriate behaviour noticed and praised or rewarded?	
Are learners involved in setting their own targets and monitoring their own progress?	

Good practice

Children with special educational needs are continuously having their learning needs addressed within mainstream provision, where a child experiencing learning difficulties will progress at an unpredictable level and therefore should be provided with a range of strategies to aid them in their learning. Children with special educational needs are often faced with a wide range of barriers to their learning, which can often include:

- a short attention span;
- poor organisational skills;
- being unable to retain information;
- having limited interest in an activity.

When considering supporting a child with special educational needs we must look at the range of different learning styles and consider how to effectively support them with a wide range of interactive processes. We must ensure we are providing a consistent and structured approach to their learning, while clarifying what is expected through checking understanding in discussion with the learner.

Sensory stimulation and cognitive learning are two learning styles that overlap in many ways and revolve around an active style which is undoubtedly suitable for all children with SEN and can be effectively used within the classroom. It is not so much about us changing how we do things rather than recognising how many different styles of teaching and learning are available to us and to the learners.

When considering learning styles for children with SEN we must first look at both the learning styles of the individual and the teaching styles within the classroom.

Sensory learning involves using visual, auditory, tactile and kinaesthetic activities to enhance learning and is based upon the theory that effective learning occurs when our senses are stimulated. Using these learning styles when supporting children with SEN ensures we are aiming to reach every child in relation to the process they may use to learn. In doing this we should be providing a more inclusive environment, not just for children with special needs but for each individual child within the classroom. In researching learning styles Prashing (2004, p105) found that

> nearly all of our presently used teaching methods rely heavily on visual and auditory skills of teachers and students alike, for young children and primary pupils it is very much acceptable that they involve their hands a lot, have large amounts of learning materials and they are allowed to 'play' with things during the learning process.

Being flexible and attempting a larger variety of activities to ensure all children stay focused and involved within lessons and group work enhances learning. It is often appropriate to use visual stimuli such as timetables, routines and instruction diagrams for children with SEN as the pressure on the child can be diminished when they do not have to keep asking for instructions, which often causes embarrassment in front of peers.

Cognitive learning focuses on the importance of experience, using this as the basis of learning and providing children with the opportunity to use the knowledge they have gained to solve problems. The cognitive style of learning provides children with new experiences, helping them to make sense of the world around them. Stewart (2004, p10) believed that learning can be more effective if the learner is actively involved in the primary construction of understanding; this then gives those supporting the learner an opportunity to let go and allow their pupil to realise their own capabilities. This style of learning opens up avenues for children to use exploration and be active in their learning. They are given the chance to collaborate in small groups and take part in discussions; working in this way also gives opportunity to group students of different abilities to help support children with learning difficulties. References are often made to collaboration within classrooms of children of different abilities and how placing children with learning difficulties in one group can limit their resources. Varying classroom organisation and mixing groups can help children with learning difficulties, not only by peer support but also they may find the materials much more accessible for their style of learning.

One of the most important aspects of supporting children with SEN is to ensure that their self-esteem needs are fully addressed. This can then enhance the confidence and motivation of pupils who are struggling to achieve. In doing this it is important to consider that the impact of a 'Can Do' classroom with an emphasis on achievement through a variety of activities, not always academic, can have a positive impact on learning. In achieving this, children can often benefit from the introduction of a designated Key Worker, usually the class TA or regular voluntary worker, who would use their judgement in conjunction with the class teacher to initiate extra activities when necessary for those children identified as having low self-esteem. By working together in this way we approached intervention through identifying needs other than academic, creating a positive environment. Through this we allow children to make valued and respected contributions using interactive sharing and learning. This then motivates pupils and encourages them to apply these skills to their learning. Jarvis (2005) talks about Maslow's theory that self-esteem is a more basic need than intellectual interest and so to stimulate the self-esteem creates the motivation needed to learn. Jarvis (2005) also discusses how motivation effects interaction with peers and can affect the balance of the classroom. This is the most important thing that we are addressing through supporting learners through self-esteem activities, allowing us to focus upon motivation and self-awareness. In doing this we provide children of all abilities with opportunities to display their own qualities and strengths, allowing them to reflect upon themselves.

CHAPTER SUMMARY

- Inclusion is a concept and a process that involves change to improve the cohesiveness and acceptance of all in society whether in school or outside it. TAs play a vital role in increasing inclusiveness in practice in schools and enhancing the culture of inclusivity in schools.
- Inclusion can relate to pupils with SEN but it is wider than that and refers to the inclusion of all groups and individuals who may be deemed by some to be 'different' and 'outside'.
- A positive attitude to pupils with SEN is crucial to this process of inclusion, where differences are not seen as problems.
- Team work and collaboration is essential for the inclusion of all pupils and staff.
- Pupils with SEN need to be assessed for individual learning styles and their work planned to harmonise with those styles to maximise learning.
- Pupils with SEN may have low self-esteem and this needs to be addressed to enhance the pupil's chance of success.

REFERENCES

Booth, T., Ainscow, M., Black-Hawkins, K., Vaughan, M. and Shaw, L. (2002) *Index for Inclusion*. Bristol: Centre for Studies in Inclusive Education.

DES (2011) *Support and Aspiration: A new approach to special educational needs and disability – A consultation*. London: DES.

DfES (2006) *Leading on Intervention*. London: DfES.

DFES (2009) *Lamb Inquiry – special educational needs and parental confidence*. London: DfES.

Jarvis, M. (2005) *The Psychology of Effective Learning and Teaching*. Cheltenham: Nelson Thornes.

Office for Standards in Education (Ofsted) (2001) Evaluating educational inclusion HMI 235 e-publication. Available online at: www.ofsted.gov.uk/publications

Prashing, B. (2004) *The Power of Diversity: New ways of learning and teaching through learning styles*. Stafford: Network Educational Press.

Richards, G. and Armstrong, F. (2008) *Key Issues for Teaching Assistants: Working in diverse and inclusive classrooms.* London: RoutldgeFalmer.

Sorsby, C. (2004) Forging and strengthening alliances: learning support staff and the challenge of inclusion, in F. Armstrong and M. Moore (eds) *Action Research for Inclusive Education: Changing places, changing practices, changing minds.* London: RoutledgeFalmer.

Stewart, M. (2004) Learning through research: an introduction to the main theories of learning. *JMU Learning and Teaching Press,* 4 (1), 6–14.

Thomas, G. and Loxley, A. (2001) *Deconstructing Special Education and Constructing Inclusion.* Buckingham: Open University Press.

UNESCO (1994) The Salamanca Statement and Framework for Action on Special Needs Education. World Conference on Special Needs Education, Access and Quality. Available online at www.unesco.org/education/pdf/SALAMA_E.PDF (accessed 2/3/12).

Useful websites

The Centre for Studies on Inclusive Education (CSIE): (www.csie.org.uk)

Further reading

Richards, G. and Armstrong, F. (2008) *Key Issues for Teaching Assistants: Working in diverse and inclusive classrooms* (London: RoutledgeFalmer).

6 BEHAVIOUR FOR LEARNING

Alexis Moore and Joanne Sutcliffe

CHAPTER OBJECTIVES

By the end of this chapter you will have:

- gained an understanding of the developmental stages of behaviour;
- understood the importance of behaviour for learning and 'learning behaviour';
- identified strategies to enable you to promote positive behaviour;
- started to develop an understanding of moderate and specific learning difficulties.

LINKS TO **HLTA** STANDARDS

1. Demonstrate the positive values, attitudes and behaviour they expect from children and young people.

2. Understand the key factors that affect children's and young people's learning and progress.

3. Use effective strategies to promote positive behaviour.

These standards cannot be viewed in isolation as each one is interrelated. Consistently modelling the types of behaviours expected of the children that you work with will contribute to a positive learning environment and enable children to develop positive learning behaviours.

Introduction

Over the past 50 years, the school approach to behaviour has evolved from one that is mainly based on sanctions and punishment to one that is based on positive reinforcement and support. The role of the Teaching Assistant (TA) in supporting behaviour for learning is very important and one that is often underestimated.

The government commissioned a report published in 1989, *The Elton Report: Enquiry into discipline in schools* (DES and Welsh Office, 1989). This report forms the basis of many current guidance documents, policies and legislation in schools and settings today. The report suggested that schools should 'plan' to manage behaviour in a positive rather than a reactive way. This report also established the link between classroom management, organisation and the curriculum and found that the quality of teaching and learning has a 'significant' impact on behaviour. In 1989, when the report was written, there were very few adults working in classrooms who were not teachers, and the significant impact of the TA within the school could not have been anticipated.

Following this, in 2005, a review was commissioned by the DfES and chaired by Sir Alan Steer that resulted in *The Report of The Practitioners' Group on School Behaviour and Discipline* (DfES, 2005). The report was based on a set of six core beliefs.

- *The quality of learning, teaching and behaviour in schools [comprises] inseparable issues, and [is] the responsibility of all staff.*
- *Poor behaviour cannot be tolerated, as it is a denial of the right of the pupils to learn and teachers to teach. To enable learning to take place, preventative action is the most effective, but where this fails, schools must have clear, firm and intelligent strategies in place to help pupils manage their behaviour.*
- *There is no single solution to the problem of poor behaviour, but all schools have the potential to raise standards if they are consistent in implementing good practice in learning, teaching and behaviour management.*
- *Respect has to be given in order to be received. Parents and carers, pupils and teachers all need to operate in a culture of mutual regard.*
- *The support of parents is essential for the maintenance of good behaviour. Parents and schools each need to have a clear understanding of their rights and responsibilities.*
- *School leaders have a critical role in establishing high standards of learning, teaching and behaviour.*

(DfES, 2005)

Following the Steer Report there were a number of initiatives intended to enable schools and settings to promote positive behaviours for learning. The Primary and Secondary National Strategies focus on social and emotional aspects of learning were referred to as SEAL materials. Many of these strategies were adopted by schools and settings. New roles began to emerge in schools to support learning and behaviour; these included Learning Mentors, Behaviour and Attendance Officers, Family Support Assistants, and Behaviour Improvement programmes.

The National Strategies website was removed following the coalition government taking office in May 2010. Materials that were previously available on the National Strategies website can be accessed through the National Archives.

In 2011, the Department for Education published a document called *Behaviour and discipline in schools: A guide for head teachers and school staff* to replace previous guidance in the interim before the Education Bill progressed through the legislative process in autumn 2011. A behaviour 'expert' was appointed to advise schools, settings and practitioners on behaviour. There are interesting changes in language and vocabulary used in different policy and guidance documents. For example, the terms 'sanctions' and 'punishments'.

Models for behaviour management have been based on behaviourist theories, such as those of Skinner, Pavlov and Thorndyke. Behaviourist theorists suggest that all behaviour is learned and is subject to conditioning. Consequently, desired behaviours can be encouraged by reward and undesired behaviours can be discouraged by punishment. Other theorists suggest that behaviour is dependent on social conditions and how individuals interact. For more information regarding theories relating to behaviour and learning, see Watkinson (2003), Hryniewicz (2007) and Bentham (2006).

PRACTICAL TASK

Obtain a copy of policy relating to behaviour in school.

- Identify language relating to positive aspects of behaviour.
- Identify agreed rewards and sanctions.
- Do you follow the agreed systems?
- How do you model positive behaviour for learning in school?
- What do you see your responsibility to be in promoting positive behaviours for learning?

Understanding behaviour

All learning behaviour is rooted in relationships and positive relationships facilitate learning.

Following the EPPI-centre review (Powell and Tod, 2004, p82) of how learning theories explain behaviour in school contexts, the team of reviewers held the view that the 'fostering of learning behaviour' or 'behaviour for learning' was the foundation of effective behaviour management rather than 'learning to behave'.

Figure 6.1 is adapted from the EPPI-centre review. The suggestion is that all learning behaviour is dependent upon relationships. The relationship that the learner has with learning and the

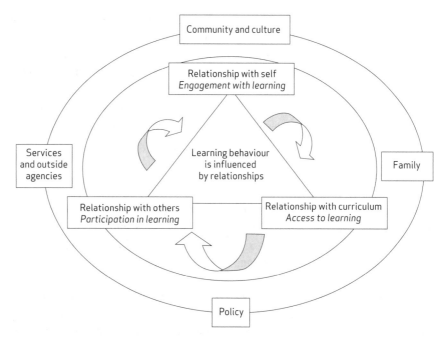

Figure 6.1: The influence of relationships on behaviour (adapted from EPPI-centre, 2004)

consequential self-image as a learner; the relationship the learner has with the curriculum and its relevance to them personally; and the relationship the learner has with others, including peers and adults. While a pupil's learning behaviour is influenced by relationships, in turn these relationships are influenced by other factors, such as family, policy and other agencies.

While, for the majority of children, the balance between these factors means that children develop good behaviours for learning, there are undoubtedly groups of vulnerable children for whom the balance changes. As such, we as educators need to be aware of any external influences affecting an individual's 'learning behaviour' and of the past experiences and perceptions the child may have. In this way the holistic learning needs of pupils can be addressed.

Developmental stages in learning behaviours

Learning to behave in a socially acceptable manner is something that is usually recognised as having 'milestones' linked to social development. One would not expect a teenager to respond to being told they could not go and play in the garden in the same way as a two-year-old, although some parents of teenagers may disagree.

The Statutory Framework for the Early Years Foundation Stage (EYFS) (DCSF, 2008) has four themes that express key principles underpinning effective practice in EYFS.

1. A Unique Child – every child is a competent learner who can be resilient, capable, confident and self-assured.
2. Positive Relationships – children learn to be strong and independent from a base of loving and secure relationships with parents and/or a key person.
3. Enabling Environments – the environment plays a key role in supporting and extending children's development and learning.
4. Learning and Development – children develop and learn in different ways and at different rates, and all areas of learning and development are equally important and interconnected.

From this, it may be assumed that learning behaviours are embedded across the curriculum and throughout the Early Years' settings (DCSF, 2008).

A new baby learns to expect responses to certain behaviours very quickly as its social development skills start to develop. The impact of modelled behaviours from adults and peers is crucial to development (DCSF, 2008).

By nursery and reception age, children build a stronger identity of self and their place in the world. They start to recognise the importance of social rules and customs; they develop understanding and tolerance, and learn how to be more controlled in their own behaviour. Social skills are further developed when playing in small groups; there is a developing understanding of sensitivity to the needs, views and feelings of others and of cause, effect and consequences. Children understand what is right and wrong and why. At this stage children express needs and feelings in appropriate ways (DCSF, 2008).

When children have difficulties in their lives or face adversity, it may be that some of these stages are not fully developed. When dealing with behaviours that are not age appropriate, it can be useful to think of these stages and how you would respond if the pupil were a younger child. In these cases, children need some guidance as to the appropriate responses when they are calm, for example 'I know you are angry but when you are screaming and shouting, it is difficult to understand what you are angry about. When you are calm, you can tell me and we can find a solution.'

The Tickell Review of Early Years Foundation Stage commissioned by the Government in 2010 made recommendations for change to be implemented in September 2012. The emphasis on healthy development and learning for early years remains the focus, with three prime areas identified as the foundations of personal, social and emotional development, communication and language and physical development. However, there will always be situations where behaviours are displayed that are outside the expectations of the age and stage of development.

Challenging behaviours

Nutbrown and Clough (2006, p28) suggest that challenging behaviours in the Early Years are defined by the environment in which the behaviours take place. So in an Early Years environment children are encouraged to access the outdoors, go to the toilet when it is needed, make choices for independent learning during the session, and communicate ideas with their peers and adults at most times of the day. These types of behaviour are clearly not acceptable in the more formal setting of Year 6 and, if they were displayed, may be described as 'challenging'. Acceptable behaviours relate to the development of social skills and relationships.

Just as current initiatives in education suggest that identifying the 'What's in it for me?' (WIIFM) aspects of learning for pupils will increase motivation, this can be a useful analogy for practitioners to think about when presented with challenging behaviours. The skill in understanding behaviours is what motivates a pupil to behave in a particular way. Dinkmeyer and Dreikurs (2000) suggest that all behaviour has a purpose and is linked with a desire to belong. They describe four common patterns of behaviour that relate to attention, power, revenge and helplessness or inadequacy; the individual may not be aware of the purpose of the behaviour, but the practitioner should understand that the pupil or young person may behave in a particular way in order to provoke a reaction or response. This is a key element in developing an understanding of behaviour. For example, the child who needs attention will not necessarily be able to distinguish between 'positive' and negative' attention as either way will involve an interaction with the adult.

A key aspect to managing behaviour is to develop a proactive approach that plans for positive behaviour, rather than always having to adopt a reactive response to both positive and negative behaviours. When you react to behaviour it can often be an instinctive response, but this is sometimes necessary. For example, if there is a dangerous situation that you see about to happen, you may shout 'STOP!' to avoid that potential danger. However, it would be hoped that this would then be followed by an explanation of why you raised your voice and what the possible consequences could have been of the dangerous behaviour.

REFLECTIVE TASK

Think of a time when you 'reacted' to a behavioural situation rather than 'responded'. What was the context? What happened?

Would the outcome have been the same if your behaviours had been different?

Learning environment

There are many aspects to creating a learning environment that incorporate planning for positive behaviours. The establishment of routines, rules and rituals can provide security for pupils when linked to rights and responsibilities. Rogers (2007, p126) suggests that a key factor of behaviour management is the language we use and consideration of the following principles.

- Educators must be confident in dealing with behaviours and be aware of both verbal and non-verbal communications. What do you think your body language would convey to pupils if you were standing with your arms folded and your foot tapping?
- A calm, controlled approach should be adopted and you should ensure that you are calm before trying to calm a pupil.
- Language should focus on the behaviour rather than be a verbal attack on the individual.
- Instructions, requests and commands should be brief and focus on behaviour.
- Pupils need to be given enough 'take-up time' when possible to comply with instructions, even if this means ignoring some secondary behaviours in the meantime.
- Ensure that correcting behaviours is balanced with encouragement and there is an expectation that working relationships will be re-established.
- Concentrate and focus on the 'primary behaviours' and 'primary issues' relating to rules, responsibilities and rights rather than being distracted by the secondary behaviours that may be displayed by pupils, such as sighing, shrugging shoulders, having to have the last word, etc.
- Make sure that you are consistent in your approach, having an agreed level of sanctions and rewards.
- In line with school policy, involve other people, other adults within school and parents for both positive and negative aspects of behaviour.
- Maintain the respect and dignity of pupils by using the least intrusive approach; this can avoid situations escalating and can work within the agreed level of responses, rewards and sanctions.
- Provide support for pupils to make reparation and reconciliation in order that this becomes a recognised part of the process.

As adults within the school setting, it can be argued that it is our responsibility to model the desired behaviours. If we expect a calm, consistent environment with clarity about what is, and is not, acceptable behaviour within that environment, then we have to demonstrate that we too follow this code. For many children and young people within our care, their school or setting may be one of the few environments that consistently display these values.

CASE STUDY 1

Scenario 1

In Class A, the children come into school, hang up their coats, take their reading book bags into the classroom and put them in their trays. Some children get activities out and start to play; others sit on the carpet waiting for the teacher. When the teacher comes to the carpet to take the register, she tells the children doing activities to put them away. In doing so, they put away the activities that are on the table ready for the next session. The TA is getting the book bags from the trays and is changing the books for the children. There is a pile of bags she cannot deal with as there are queries about the next book. Charlie is engrossed in making a tower and, in an effort to get him to come to the carpet for register, his friend starts to dismantle the tower. Charlie shouts at him to stop and then hits him and both children are now crying. The teacher leaves the carpet to deal with the disagreement. The TA starts to take the register. The activities that children are sent to are incomplete and children are not on task.

Scenario 2

In Class B, the Foundation Stage practitioner has developed a self-registration system for the mornings. Children find their name and photograph card on a table and 'velcro' it to the register list displayed at child height on the wall. They put their book bag in a labelled box and the TA talks to them about the books they have read. There are a number of activities out on the tables that children can access freely. Some of these activities have a cartoon alligator placed on top. The children know this is a signal that this equipment is not to be played with before the first carpet time of the morning. There are a number of cartoon alligators available for children to use if they are in the middle of a model when it is time to tidy up for the first session. This avoids upset and allows children to sustain concentration. Children are given a 'five-minute' cue time for coming to the carpet, which allows them to tidy their area, put pictures away and put alligators on tasks that they want to keep; it also encourages collaboration and helping each other. Children are ready on the carpet for the teaching input, which starts with a 'Well done' for coming into the classroom sensibly and a short discussion about choosing activities.

REFLECTIVE TASK

Which classroom, in case study 1, would you rather be in if you were five years old? Why? What can you do to make your classroom a supportive environment that encourages behaviour for learning?

A key factor in behaviour for learning is planning for positive behaviour outcomes. As can be seen from the examples in case study 1, the responsibility is on the adults within schools and settings to create a learning environment in which pupils are safe and secure. Pupils should be given opportunities to develop independence and scaffolds within which they can make choices and develop positive attitudes to learning. In this way children can 'learn' acceptable behaviours.

Creating routines and rituals within the classroom will enable children to know they are 'doing the right thing'. Positive re-enforcement of this behaviour by adults and peers encourages these behaviours to be perpetuated and frees time for adults to deal with the important issues of developing positive relationships and learning rather than reacting to and dealing with behavioural incidents. This is particularly important for pupils who display challenging behaviours. By providing a predictable, positive learning environment, children are more likely to be able to conform rather than having to 'guess' what the teacher/practitioner wants.

Moderate learning difficulties and the impact on behaviour for learning

There is a range of differing perspectives on the terminology used to describe learning difficulties and additional needs. Many children with moderate learning difficulties may also be suffering from low levels of self-esteem and lack of motivation. As pupils may believe they are likely to fail before they begin, many may refuse to attempt new work. For those who are supported by TAs there is a possibility that pupils may become over-reliant on them to help them with tasks. This may lead to pupil's needing much more encouragement and praise to persuade them to attempt new challenges which are within their capability and develop greater independence.

Pupils who have moderate learning difficulties (MLD), sometimes referred to as 'global learning difficulties', usually have a statement of SEN or will be included on the school's or setting's special needs/inclusion register at 'School Action Plus'. This group of children comprises the majority of children on the SEN register in mainstream schools (Graf and Birch, 2009).

For these children, there are often associated difficulties in accessing the curriculum in terms of relevance, developing relationships with peers and maintaining a positive self-image as a learner. The triangle of relationships affecting behaviour in Figure 6.1 (p66) is particularly pertinent for children with significant learning needs. Children with any additional learning needs, and particularly children who have speech and language delay, may need alternative strategies in order to assist them in developing a positive self-image and making good choices with behaviour.

There is a number of strategies that can be used to avoid conflict and encourage independence. These may include using picture cues to describe the desired behaviours, using picture cues to give structure and order to the day, following routines and rituals, and encouraging children to predict what is going to happen next so that they develop personal independence. Often, limited choice can be accompanied by a physical cue. For example, a TA may hold out two hands: (holding out the right hand) 'Do you want to tidy up your work space by yourself?' or (holding out the left hand) 'Would you like me to help you?' The child can then touch the hand to indicate the choice.

By creating a positive learning environment, potential difficulties with behaviour for learning can be avoided. To support more challenging behaviour, the following strategies may be useful.

- Use scale pictures from 1 to 10 to help children describe how they are feeling, particularly when angry.
- Teach techniques for reducing stress, anger and anxiety.
- Reinforce positive messages regarding behaviour, e.g. 'Well done for letting Simon be first in the line', 'You were very patient when you let Harry use the pencil sharpener first.' Also,

make observations regarding other children's behaviours, e.g. 'Harry was very kind when he asked you to play tag with him.'

- Role play social situations that can cause conflict or upset to rehearse responses, e.g. 'If you do not want to play, say No thank you.'
- Give clear, limited options and choices for behaviour.
- Be consistent; understand choices for behaviour, but the agreed consequences of the choice should still stand.
- Find solutions rather than focus on problems, and encourage children to think through actions and reparation, e.g. 'How can you make things better after you pushed Simon out of the line?'

Specific learning difficulties and the impact on behaviour for learning

With specific learning difficulties (SpLD), we examine the concern that, if strategies are not developed to enhance learning, behavioural difficulties may arise. There are conflicting perspectives concerning the terminology used to describe learning and behavioural difficulties. Currently, the DCSF[RM4] uses the definitions described earlier in this chapter. The debate on the labelling of special, specific, moderate and additional educational needs is further discussed in the chapter on inclusion (Chapter 5). The SpLDs discussed within this chapter are:

- dyslexia;
- dyscalculia;
- dyspraxia.

Learning difficulties that could lead to behavioural difficulties

Pupils with dyslexia, dyscalculia and dyspraxia may never display behavioural difficulties or problems. However, it is important to understand that these can arise and can lead to significant behavioural issues if they are not managed carefully. Students can become frustrated and annoyed, which may discourage them from learning and may lead others to become unable to learn.

Dyslexia

Dyslexia is an SpLD that impedes the learning of literacy skills; that is, a dyslexic person has problems learning to read, write and spell. This problem with managing verbal codes in memory is neurologically based, as in the way 'the brain is organised connected and used' (Hryniewicz, 2007, p283). Other symbolic systems, such as mathematics and reading music, can also be affected. Dyslexia can occur at any level of intellectual ability. It can accompany, but is not a result of, lack of motivation, emotional disturbance and/or sensory impairment. An individual is identified as dyslexic when a significant discrepancy exists between intellectual ability and reading performance without an apparent alternative cause.

The following suggestions may help deal with aspects of this difficulty to ensure that we promote positive behaviour for learning.

- Provide multi-sensory teaching and structured learning, always building upon prior learning.
- Ensure plenty of practice is provided in relation to areas of work and slowly build up the development of these areas, which may lead to giving smaller, more manageable tasks. Ensure that all instructions are short and clear.
- Allow extra time for answering questions as pupils may need to integrate and combine various subjects.
- When producing work, use large fonts, relevant coloured paper and mind maps, and utilise look, say, write, cover, check.

Dyscalculia

Dyscalculia is defined by Sousa as a condition that leaves individuals with a difficulty in conceptualising numbers, number relationships, outcomes of numerical operations, and estimation (2007, p143). This could include a difficulty in acquiring simple number concepts, an inability to grasp innate number facts and procedures, and no confidence in the answers or methods they choose, even if correct. Pupils will have an impaired sense of number size, will have difficulties comparing numbers and will have problems with estimating numbers in a collection. It is clear that, if pupils struggle with mathematics, behavioural problems can arise, as often specific, correct answers are needed that they are unable to provide; and an anxiety about mathematics leads to problems, for example pupils wanting to avoid the subject at all costs.

The following suggestions may help deal with aspects of this difficulty to ensure that we promote positive behaviour for learning.

- Keep worksheets uncluttered and well spaced and, wherever possible, include clear steps and instructions. Keep any worksheet as multi-sensory as possible.
- Ensure that the student is aware of the mathematical concept, as many will learn sequences by rote and then find it impossible to use these when not in the specific order they have learned. Pupils with dyscalculia will also have problems making their own sequencing instructions, so plenty of support is needed.
- Use as many visual aids as possible, as most pupils will have a poor sense of direction, will have difficulty in telling the time and will find it hard to handle money. This means providing lots of real-life experiences linked to these mathematical activities and, wherever possible, using repetition.

Dyspraxia

Dyspraxia is when messages are not properly transmitted to the body due to an immaturity in the brain that causes problems with motor co-ordination (Brownhill, 2007). Dyspraxia is a disability, but is not apparent to others, which can be both an advantage and a disadvantage to the individual. Aspects of dyspraxia may be interpreted as behavioural problems, but are in fact characteristics of it. This may include younger children becoming aggressive due to lack of communication skills, thereby having difficulty establishing friendships. This could lead to the impression that the pupil is a loner and an introvert. It is often difficult to reason with a pupil with dyspraxia, and temper tantrums can be common. Other difficulties include speech problems and difficulty answering questions, although answers are known. This could result in the pupil being seen as uncooperative. Pupils may have reading and writing difficulties and an inability to hold a pen or pencil correctly, although this may not be a problem on other occasions.

Although there is no cure for dyspraxia, specialist help can promote a greater chance of improvement.

- Occupational therapists and physiotherapists can help the individual overcome many difficulties, although many skills we take for granted will never become automatic for a dyspraxic child.
- Extra help in school will help teach these skills, which can then help with overcoming other difficulties.
- If content is the more desired outcome for a lesson and presentation is less important, it is essential that collaboration, including full support, is given with writing, drawing and the plan of work.

Aspects of social, emotional and behavioural difficulties that could have an effect upon learning

Attention deficit disorders

Attention deficit disorder (ADD) and attention deficit hyperactivity disorder (ADHD) can affect children at all stages of education and are more common in boys. Pupils with ADD/ADHD often display signs of dyspraxia as well. If pupils with ADD/ADHD are not offered specific support in relation to their learning, this could severely impair their development and opportunities for learning. A lack of support could also lead to behavioural problems, which could then have an effect upon the learning of others within that educational environment. Aspects of ADD/ADHD that may be misinterpreted as behavioural problems can include struggling to follow instructions and complete set tasks, being easily distracted and forgetful, and having difficulty listening when spoken to. Pupils with ADD/ADHD often fidget, squirm and can't sit still. They may also be unable to stop talking and, annoyingly, will constantly interrupt others. The pupils may also blurt out answers without waiting to be asked, as they have difficulty awaiting their turn and will act impulsively without thinking about consequences.

It is extremely important initially to pinpoint the difficulties an individual may be experiencing, as support time can be wasted and the individual can feel frustrated if support is given in an area where few difficulties emerge (Sousa, 2007). Other suggestions to help deal with this difficulty include the following.

- Keep timetables and lessons as predictable as possible by creating a daily routine.
- Set short achievable tasks and be very specific with any instructions for tasks.
- Give immediate rewards, including praise and attention when behaviour is good, and make clear, reasonable requests for behaviour.
- Keep rules simple and clear, set boundaries that are easily understood and ensure consistency in managing the pupil. This includes the use of rewards and sanctions.

- Plan learning to gradually lengthen the pupil's concentration and ability to focus on tasks.
- It is important to communicate with the pupil on a one-to-one basis and ensure that this is not interrupted by others.

Autism Spectrum

Autism Spectrum is often used to describe disorders that are currently classified as pervasive developmental disorders. Pervasive developmental disorders include Autistic Disorder and Asperger's Disorder as well as Childhood Disintegrative Disorder, Rett's Disorder and Pervasive Development Disorder (which are not otherwise specified). Autism is a life-long developmental disability that prevents individuals from properly understanding what they see, hear and otherwise sense, which can result in severe problems with social relationships, communication and behaviour. Children with autism will have severe delay in language development and in understanding social relationships. They will have inconsistent patterns of sensory responses and uneven patterns of intellectual functioning. Autistic children will also show a marked restriction in activities and interests. Asperger's syndrome is characterised by severe and sustained impairment in social interaction, and the development of restricted and repetitive patterns of behaviour, interests and activities (Sousa, 2007). Pupils with Asperger's will often be unaware of others' feelings, so are unable to carry on with a 'give and take' conversation. This can lead to an inability to develop peer relationships that are appropriate to the developmental level. Any changes in routines and transition can cause upset.

It is important to remember that any misbehaviour is not personal and the following suggestions can help deal with this difficulty.

- Ensure that the individual is organised for their learning, which can include breaking things down into smaller steps.
- Be as concrete as possible and be aware of literal speech. This may be avoiding excess verbal communication.
- Reduce stress by decreasing unusual or difficult behaviours and keep any changes to routine minimal.
- Facial expressions (or other social cues) may not work with children who lie within the autistic spectrum.

Conduct disorder

Conduct disorder (CD) refers to a group of behavioural and emotional problems in which individuals act towards others in a destructive way (Sousa, 2007). Individuals with this disorder have great difficulty following rules and behaving in a socially acceptable way. Behavioural issues include showing aggression towards people and animals, including bullying, threatening and intimidation. There is a deliberate destruction of property and individuals with CD may also steal, as long as there is no confrontation. A pupil may also show signs of deceitfulness and lying, and will display serious violations of rules, both at home and school.

Specialist help is needed to deal with this disorder.

- Comprehensive and specific help is often needed, which may have to take place in different settings.

- Behaviour therapy and psychotherapy are often needed to help with this disorder. Treatment is a longer-term process, as in most cases patterns of behaviour and attitude need to be altered.

Oppositional defiance disorder

Oppositional defiance disorder (ODD) is constant disobedience and an opposition to various authoritative persons, including parents, teachers and other adults (Sousa, 2007, p168). However, the basic rights of others are respected and age-appropriate rules are not violated. This disorder displays several behavioural problems, which can include frequent temper tantrums. Pupils with ODD may also have unnecessary and sometimes extreme arguments with adults, and these may come from an active defiance and refusal to comply with adult requests. The pupils will upset and annoy people deliberately; however, they will also be easily annoyed by others. They may also be quick-tempered and become easily upset, and will show frequent anger and resentment towards others, which often leads to revenge seeking. There will also be no responsibility taken for their mistakes or misbehaviour.

There are various suggestions to help deal with this disorder.

- A behavioural modification programme is needed, which can be developed in the classroom. This may involve:
  - ensuring behaviour to be observed is clearly specified in terms of 'actions and performance';
  - establishing a 'baseline' so that any modification in behaviour can be measured;
  - setting goals that encourage academic and social development;
  - determining signals and prompts that help direct individuals to behave in a particular manner;
  - determining positive reinforcements for appropriate behaviour and, when necessary, punishments, which can only stop bad behaviours, not promote desirable ones;
  - evaluating the behavioural modification programme to determine success and ways forward.
- It is important to give a lot of praise and encouragement when the pupil is co-operative and working well. This may be for small areas of improvement in the first instance; however, these could be huge steps for the pupil. For example, praise for sitting down when asked may seem pointless to others, but could be very important for the pupil. It important to note also that this doesn't have to be done in front of the whole class.
- There is little point in arguing with the pupil. It is more important to show them that there will not be any confrontational engagement, even if this means removal of the pupil or the rest of the group (as the learning needs of others have to be met). The situation is easier to deal with when there is a calm environment and then discussions can take place linked to the behaviour modification programme.

Obsessive compulsive disorder

Obsessive compulsive disorder (OCD) is an anxiety disorder in which a person has unreasonable thoughts, fears or worries and tries to manage this by performing ritual activities in the hope that these will reduce the anxiety. Sousa indicates that this disorder involves patterns of repeated thoughts and behaviours that are impossible to control or to stop (2007, p165). Areas include an extreme preoccupation with dirt, germs or contamination, and obtrusive thoughts about violence, hurting, killing someone or self-harming. Other compulsive behaviours include checking and rechecking, following rigid rules of order and hoarding objects, as well as the repetition of words, questions, obscenities, obscene actions, sounds and music. Specialist help such as behaviour therapy and medication is normally required, and a combination of both is usually most effective.

The suggestions given in this chapter can only ever be a guide to strategies that could be adopted in order to support children in behaviour for learning and learning behaviours. Each school will have individual approaches within a national framework for behaviour and each child will have individual needs, some of which will need a more personalised response.

The key to developing positive behaviours is relationships based on mutual respect and harnessing motivation to learn. For some children, this is linked to developmental stages, and social and emotional needs that have to be addressed alongside learning. However, for all children, we would want them to develop self-management strategies and independence. Behaviour for learning is an intrinsic part of school, the curriculum and each person within the school community:

Central to the development of learning behaviour is motivation and self-discipline to move students from externally driven strategies towards the self-motivation and self-regulation needed for life-long learning and achievement (EPPI-centre, 2004, p88).

CHAPTER SUMMARY

- The quality of learning, teaching and behaviour in schools comprises inseparable issues, and is the responsibility of all staff.
- Behaviour is learned and children go through developmental stages. These may not always be age appropriate, so children need support with their behaviour.
- Behaviour for learning and learning to behave are interrelated. It is the role of educators to enable children to develop skills and understanding about positive behaviour choices.
- There is a range of strategies and approaches that can be personalised within an agreed school system to meet individual learning and behavioural needs.

REFERENCES

Bentham, S. (2006) *A Teaching Assistant's Guide to Managing Behaviour in the Classroom*. Abingdon: Routledge.

Brownhill, S. (2007) *Taking the Stress out of Bad Behaviour*. London: Continuum.

Department for Children, Schools and Families (DCSF) (2008) *Statutory Framework for the Early Years Foundation Stage* (2008) Nottingham: DCSF Publications.

Department for Education (2011) *Behaviour and Discipline: A guide for schools*. London: DfE. Available online at www.education.gov.uk/aboutdfe/advice/f0076803/behaviour-and-discipline-in-schools-a-guide-for-headteachers-and-school-staff (accessed 27/2/12).

Department for Education and Skills (DfES) (2005) *The Report of The Practitioners' Group on School Behaviour and Discipline*. London: DfES.

Department of Education and Science and the Welsh Office (1989) *The Elton Report: Enquiry into discipline in schools*. London: HMSO.

Dinkmeyer, D. and Dreikurs, R. (2000) *Encouraging Children to Learn*. Philadelphia, PA: Brunner-Routledge.

Graf, M. and Birch, A. (2009) *The Teaching Assistant's Guide to Understanding and Supporting Learning*. London: Continuum.

Hryniewicz, L. (2007) *Teaching Assistants: The complete handbook* (2nd edition). Norwich: Adamson Publishing.

Nutbrown, C. and Clough, P. (2006) *Inclusion in the Early Years*. London: Sage.

Powell, S. and Tod, J. (2004) A systematic review of how theories explain learning behaviour in school contexts. In *Research Evidence in Education Library*. London: EPPI-Centre, Social Science Research Unit, Institute of Education, University of London.

Rogers, B. (2007) *Behaviour Management: A whole school approach* (2nd edition). London: Sage.

Sousa, D. A. (2007) *How the Special Needs Brain Learns* (2nd edition). London: Corwin Press.

Watkinson, A. (2003) *The Essential Guide for Experienced Teaching Assistants* (2nd edition). London: David Fulton Publishers.

FURTHER READING

Adams, K. (2009) *Behaviour for Learning in the Primary School: Achieving QTS*. Exeter: Learning Matters.

Dix, P. (2010) *The Essential Guide to Taking Care of Behaviour* (2nd edition). Harlow: Pearson Education.

Imray, P. (2008) *Turning the Tables on Challenging Behaviour: A practitioner's perspective to transforming challenging behaviours in children, young people and adults with SLD, PMD or ASD*. London: Routledge.

Rogers, B. (2009) *How to Manage Children's Challenging Behaviour*. London: Sage.

Rogers, B. and McPherson, E. (2008) *Behaviour Management with Young Children: Crucial first steps with children 3–7 years*. London: Sage.

USEFUL WEBSITES

For current DfE publications www.education.gov.uk/publications

www.autism.org.uk

The National Strategies website closed on 31 March 2011. However, there are a number of resources that are available through the National Archives: http://webarchive.national archives.gov.uk/20110809091832/http:/teachingandlearningresources.org.uk/whole-school/social-and-emotional-aspects-learning-seal (accessed 27/10/11).

7 TEACHING AND LEARNING

Sue Faragher and Gillian Goddard

CHAPTER OBJECTIVES

By the end of this chapter you will have understood:

- the developmental, social constructivist and behaviourist approaches underpinning how children learn;
- the role that learning styles and multiple intelligences play in pupils' learning;
- the importance of a positive learning climate on motivation and learning.

LINKS TO **HLTA** STANDARDS

1. Understand the key factors that affect children's and young people's learning and progress.

2. Know how to contribute to effective personalised provision by taking practical account of diversity.

3. Understand the objectives, content and intended outcomes for learning activities in which they are involved.

4. Devise clearly structured activities that interest and motivate learners and advance their learning.

5. Advance learning when working with individuals.

6. Advance learning when working with small groups.

7. Advance learning when working with whole classes without the presence of the assigned teacher.

Introduction

In this chapter you will reflect on the theories underpinning how children learn, including developmental, social constructivist and behaviourist approaches, relating this to your own practice. Through an explanation of learning styles and multiple intelligences you will consider how knowledge of these can promote children's learning and you will reflect on the importance of a positive learning climate in promoting children's motivation and learning.

Theories of how children learn

In the late nineteenth and early twentieth centuries educational scientists equated mental ability with the ability to learn and ultimately a measure of intelligence. Alfred Binet (1857–1911) was a law graduate who became fascinated with psychology and is most widely known for his work on intelligence:

> It seems to us that in intelligence there is a fundamental faculty, the alteration or the lack of which, is of the utmost importance for practical life. This faculty is judgement . . . A person may be a moron or an imbecile if he is lacking in judgment . . . Indeed the rest of intellectual faculties seem of little importance in comparison to judgement.
>
> (Binet and Simon, 1916/1973, pp42–3)

Binet had two daughters who he researched initially to refine his view of intelligence. He was joined in his work in 1920 by Théodore Simon and together they created what is known as the Binet–Simon scale. This comprised a set of tasks that they believed, through intensive research, were typical of children's abilities at certain ages. Their aim was to be able to compare children's mental abilities with those of their peers. There was a 30-point scale of increasing difficulty and the score achieved was deemed to be the child's mental age. This, they believed, was intrinsically linked to the ability to learn.

Binet and Simon were fully aware of the limitations of their tests and did not intend to create a *scale of intelligence* (Entwistle, 1989, p141). However, the tasks scale soon became used in this way and was further developed into the formulation of an intelligence quotient (IQ).

Since this time, there has been a succession of educational theorists searching for the way in which children learn. They basically fall into two broad categories – behaviourists and constructivists.

Behaviourists believe that learning is the acquisition of any new behaviour that relies totally on the observation of this behaviour. The two types are:

- classic conditioning, which is a natural reflex action to a stimulus; Pavlov showed an example of this when he trained dogs to salivate on a signal that food was about to be brought to them;
- behavioural conditioning, when a response is reinforced – a reward or reinforcement system.

Burrhus Skinner, born in Pennsylvania in 1904, was a leading behaviourist. He believed that people learn best by being rewarded by positive responses to an action or experience or demotivated by negative responses – as illustrated in his experiment with rats. The rats, in a special cage with a press-down bar on one side, accidentally find out that, if they press the bar, a food pellet is released. They then learn to do this again and again as and when they want food. When the rat presses the bar but no food is released, the rat learns to stop pressing the bar. Critics of behaviourism, however, point out that research in this area has been done only with animals and it therefore disregards any thought processes of which humans, but not animals, are capable.

Constructivism is based on the fact that, by observing and reflecting on new experiences, we can construct our own understanding of the world and, from that, each person generates his or her own rules, which are used to make sense of those experiences. Learning is, therefore, a search for meaning and meaning requires understanding of parts and wholes: parts must be understood in the context of wholes and wholes in the context of parts: like a jigsaw puzzle, you need the pieces and you need the overall picture. It is for each individual to construct his or her own meaning rather than memorise the 'correct' answer or repeat someone else's answer.

The Swiss biologist and psychologist, Jean Piaget (1896–1980), was also very interested in the development of the child. His theory is based on the fact that children build up their own structures within the brain through their personal responses to a variety of physical experiences within their environment. He identified four hierarchical developmental stages.

1. Sensorimotor stage – the child builds up a set of concepts about reality and how it works, but does not realise that physical objects remain when out of sight.
2. Preoperational stage – the child cannot conceptualise abstractly and still needs physical and practical situations in order to make sense of new experiences.
3. Concrete operations – as the child accumulates experiences, he or she begins to explain their experiences; abstract problem solving is possible at this stage.
4. Formal operations – cognitive structures – the child is now able to reason and hypothesise, continually adjusting existing knowledge to accommodate new learning or experiences.

(www.learningandteaching.info/learning/piaget.htm 2011)

Lev Vygotsky (1896–1934), like Piaget, believed that learners moved through a hierarchical age-related scale of development. However, he insisted that learning was essentially a social activity in which learners are actively involved. His theory sees teachers as active participants in the promotion and development of learning, which he divides into two key areas.

- Specialised skill training, which involves the formation of a habit – for example, how to eat with a knife and fork, how to skip with a rope, etc.
- Activation of large areas of the brain's consciousness, involving thinking, reasoning, problem solving, investigation.

www.learning-theories.com/vygotskys-social-learning-theory.html (2011)

Constructivism would abolish a standardised curriculum in favour of a personalised one involving hands-on problem solving and open-ended questioning at all stages of development. Constructivists concentrate learning on making connections between facts and the promotion of assessment as part of the learning process rather than on standardised testing.

REFLECTIVE TASK

Think about your school or setting. Does it, in general, follow the principles of the behaviourist or social constructivist theory?

PRACTICAL TASK

Think of three differences between behaviourist and social constructivist theories. Complete the following table. The first one has been done for you.

SOCIAL CONSTRUCTIVIST	1. The child learns through problem solving
	2.
	3.
BEHAVIOURIST	1.
	2.
	3.

Indeed, it may occur in social constructivism that the teaching and learning roles may be reversed, as indicated in the following case study.

CASE STUDY 1

Three lads came to see me wanting to start a guitar club. They wanted space to do it and some support. They wanted to advertise it and run it themselves and a teacher to supervise it. It was a spur of the moment thing, but I suppose I intuitively recognised the opportunity it offered me. I volunteered to be the supervising teacher because I play the guitar myself. Badly, I have to say. As the supervising teacher I had nothing to do except keep an eye on things, watch and listen. I became a regular member. They were a million miles ahead of me in guitar technique. They recognised that pretty quickly, too, and helped me along from where I was, not from their pinnacle of expertise. Gently, but challengingly. They were excellent teachers. They taught me so much. I think I learned a bit, too, about organisation and teamwork and something about pedagogy as well.

(adapted from MacBeath and Myers, 1999)

In this case study the teacher/learner roles were reversed. The teacher felt unthreatened by the skills and knowledge of the pupils and, as a result of attending the sessions, not only increased his or her knowledge of playing the guitar, but also of organisation, teamwork and pedagogy too (MacBeath and Myers, 1999).

REFLECTIVE TASK

Why was it that the teacher in case study 1 felt unthreatened by the knowledge and skills of the children? Why do you think some teachers may feel threatened by this situation?

For effective learning, it is essential that learners take an active role in their learning, as the three boys did in case study 1. It is also important that learners know how they learn best.

PRACTICAL TASK
Complete the spider diagram: how do you learn best?

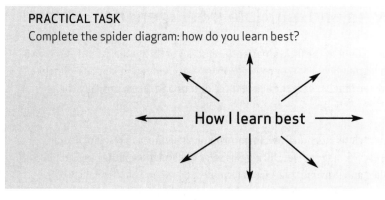

How I learn best

It is well documented that learners demonstrate increased self esteem, greater independence and ultimately higher achievement when they are involved in the development and understanding of their own learning experiences . . . When given greater opportunities for decision making and greater autonomy in their learning, they generally demonstrate greater motivation and perseverance.

(Pardoe, 2009, p8)

Lessons, therefore, should largely involve problem-solving activities. In this way, pupils can have the opportunity to investigate, research and discover information in their own way. Teachers should encourage discussion, debate, collaboration and co-operation. This further creates discussion and interaction between the pupils, who are then in control of their own learning. Discussion can be encouraged by effective questioning by the teacher. All questions should require thinking by the child; thinking extends learning.

PRACTICAL TASK
Turn these questions into 'thinking' questions. The first one is done for you.

Original question	Thinking question
What is the answer to 3764 – 1989?	Which of these is most likely to be the answer to 3764 – 1989? Why? 5753, 1775, 1795, 2775
Are drugs bad for you?	
Was Goldilocks naughty?	
Which ball bounces the highest?	
What is a complex sentence?	
Is it OK for a mother to steal food if her children are hungry?	

Learning styles and multiple intelligences

It is important to take account of the individual learning styles of the pupils. A learning style is the way in which each learner begins to concentrate on, process and retain new and difficult information. It is predetermined before the age of three or four and doesn't usually change throughout life.

Everyone has a learning style as individual as a fingerprint or signature, as a result of neural interconnection at the earliest stage of life. During this stage of development the basic architecture of the brain is established and learning styles are determined. Based on Sousa's analogy of the brain as a jungle (2006, p1), a person's preferred style is most likely to be the one they learned to use for survival as an infant, so their brain then gives it first priority for the rest of their lives. Very simply, most people understand the three modalities of visual, audio or kinaesthetic (VAK). However, many researchers, such as Ginnis (2002), see learning styles as divided into four basic areas: abstract, sequential, random and concrete, or, similarly, activists, reflectors, theorists and pragmatists (Honey and Mumford, 1992, p7). In general, most children and most adults fall somewhere between the areas and possess a combination of all four at different levels.

Concrete learners learn through doing, sensing and feeling; abstract learners learn through analysis and thought processes; active learners use a new experience in some way almost immediately; reflective learners learn through thought and reflection on experiences before acting.

Therefore, it is important for teachers to understand that some pupils like to research using books and record with writing; some like to investigate via the internet and represent their findings by a diagram or picture; some would like to represent their findings through modelling. Although it is important for pupils to have access to their own preferred style of learning, the teacher should ensure that a range of learning styles is available throughout the week, with pupils learning to work within a range of styles.

The essence of multiple intelligences is that there are many ways to learn and everyone is intelligent in their own way. With a multiple intelligence approach, intelligence is no longer reserved for those who can spell well, write well, compute difficult calculations or who have a high IQ, etc.

REFLECTIVE TASK

How would you describe 'intelligence'? Which children and adults you know are intelligent? What makes them intelligent?

CASE STUDY 2

It is a Monday morning in late autumn. The Year 3 class is timetabled for PE. It is cold out in the playground. The teacher has struggled into school with a sore throat and a headache. He is using hand signals to direct a surprisingly understanding group of shivering seven-year-olds. Mark is standing next to Thomas.

> Mark has a spelling age of 14, reading level at 3a and a numeracy score of 4c. Pretty impressive tags. Thomas can read a handful of words, has just learned to count and has difficulty writing CVC words.
>
> The teacher wants Mark to collect a ball from the equipment store. In his voiceless state, he makes two gestures, one for 'Go over there', another for 'Pick up a ball'. Mark looks at his teacher blankly. In the best tradition of communication gone astray, the teacher makes the same signals again, only slower and with more detail. Mark still doesn't know what to do when the hands move for a third time. But Thomas, who has been watching all this time, turns to Mark and says, 'He wants you to go over there and get a ball.'
>
> (Fleetham, 2006, p12)

REFLECTIVE TASK

In case study 2, who is more intelligent? Why?

Learning climate and motivation

It is vital to create a classroom where pupils are eager to learn, to discover what they don't know and where each day they can celebrate their successes; to create an atmosphere in which pupils feel safe to 'fail' and an atmosphere where 'I don't know' or 'I don't understand' is celebrated as a new opportunity to learn. Teachers need to build into pupils a sense of security – a safe haven. They need to hand over the learning to the pupils and support this by facilitating learning opportunities throughout each day – by scaffolding the learning less and less, as is suggested by Vygotsky's Zone of Proximal Development (1978). This can be seen as a continuum whereby the teacher supports the learner considerably at the outset. Eventually, the child needs the support of the teacher less and less.

An analogy for this would be learning to drive. At the start, the learner driver needs full support from a driving instructor. However, as the skill is practised, the learner driver needs the support of the instructor less and less until they can pass their driving test and are deemed qualified to drive. It involves developing a classroom in which the learner is responsible for his or her own learning – following a 'constructivist model' (Clarke, 2003, p5). Teachers need to surrender control of the learning while still supporting and aiding the learning process. Teachers should be facilitators of learning rather than instructors, understanding the needs of the pupil implicitly. It is here that Abraham Maslow's Hierarchy of Needs (1943) is still very important today.

Maslow believed that the success of the learning environment was a vital factor in pupils' self-esteem and motivation to learn, and, in order for pupils to be at optimum learning capacity, all needs must be addressed.

- Physiological needs of the pupil – the needs of the body. This refers to having access to the toilet, to food and drink, etc. As with adults, if the mind is concentrating on the fact that the body is hungry, thirsty or in need of a break or a visit to the toilet, learning is not going to take place; energies are focused on the physiological needs of the body.
- Safety needs – the need to feel secure, and that there is stability, familiarity and protection.

Figure 7.1: Hierarchy of Needs (Maslow, 1943)

- Belonging needs – pupils need to feel that they belong, that they are accepted as part of the class, the year group and the school, and that they have friends. When they feel accepted, the brain will be released from the reptilian mode and be able to move to the limbic system, where the emotions, self-identity and values are uppermost. This is the area of the brain that controls long-term memory and attention.
- Esteem needs – all pupils need to feel that they are valued, respected and recognised and appreciated within the group; that every pupil has an important part to play in the team; and that all can be successful.

It is when all these areas are fulfilled that the pupil is ready to start to learn and to become more independent in their learning.

Therefore, the teacher needs to address the physical needs of the pupils – the need for regular breaks, for movement or brain gym, for water and food, for comfort of their workplace, and for the accommodation of different learning styles. Teachers need to accept pupil autonomy and initiative, allowing pupils to engage in discussion, debate and collaboration; and to ask open-ended questions and enquire why, how, where, what if, tell me more, explain further, etc.

CASE STUDY 3

A happy eight-year-old girl skipped to find her father, who was picking her up at the end of the school day. She chattered away to him about the fun she had had until she noticed that her dad was quiet. 'What is the matter?' she asked. 'I am very sorry,' her father said softly, 'I am afraid your rabbit has died during the day.' The little girl was devastated. She had had her rabbit as long as she could remember. Every day after school she fed her rabbit and played with him. Her evening was spent very solemnly, not knowing what to do, how to feel, what to say. Very sad, she went to bed but found herself tossing and turning all night. As a result, in the morning, she was late getting up. She had to miss breakfast and could not find the homework she had done the night before. Her mum was trying to hurry her as she was going to be late for school. She quickly put on her shoes and coat and reluctantly left the house. She was rushing so much that soon she tripped and went crashing to the ground. Her knee was badly grazed and blood was trickling down her leg.

REFLECTIVE TASK

How do you think the little girl in case study 3 was feeling when she arrived at the school door? How would you feel in that situation? Is she ready to go into class and start her lessons? Why? What would you do?

Other factors affecting learning

According to Clarke (2005) the strategy that makes the most impact on learning is effective feedback. This is feedback that celebrates 'not knowing' as an opportunity for learning new things. In the case of young children, teachers could develop an area where children's new learning is acknowledged, such as a tree with leaves of new learning. Both oral and written feedback should contain a celebration of what is achieved and an area that could be improved in future. It is important, too, to allow the children the opportunity to assess their own and others' work. Children from a very young age are able to articulate what they like about their own or others' work and what they think could be done better the next time.

Some researchers insist that physical exercise plays a large part in making the brain ready to learn (Franklin Institute, 2004). Studies of the cerebellum (thought to be concerned with motor function) have now revealed that it is closely associated with spatial perception, language, attention, emotion, decision making and memory (Dommett et al., 2011). The cerebellum forms only 10 per cent of the brain, but possesses over half of the brain's neurons (Dommett et al., 2011). Movement and learning are, therefore, in a continual and complex interplay (Dommett et al., 2011). Biologically, if a person is seated for 15 to 20 minutes, the blood flows to the feet and bottom. By standing up or moving about, the blood can be recirculated and, within just one minute, the flow of blood to the brain can increase by 15 per cent (Dommett et al., 2011). It is, therefore, very important to have a classroom where the children are frequently able to move, to do a brain gym exercise, to be able to see, hear and do, and to learn through a variety of ways.

With the development of MRI scanning (Magnetic Resonance Imaging) in the 1990s great advances have been made in our understanding of the way the brain works and this has enabled researchers to explore learning processes by measuring and seeing brain function as children and adults are undertaking learning tasks. This had led to an expansion of education strategies for teachers and psychologists based on neuroscience and can be investigated further at the following sources (Royal Society, 2011; Jensen 2008).

The essence of learning

With the recent development of initiatives such as assessment for learning, personalised learning, accelerated learning, emotional literacy, and the social and emotional aspects of learning (SEAL) project, it is difficult to know which is effective in enhancing pupil learning, and which of the above initiatives or combinations of these or other initiatives to adopt. In essence, the above strategies are extremely similar. 'Assessment for learning' is about providing a safe, stimulating environment where pupils are confident learners and take control of their own targets for improvement.

'Personalised learning' is realising that one size does not fit all, and that equal is not fair. It is being able to allow pupils to feel that they are being given the opportunity to fulfil their view of their potential, identifying and responding to individual learning styles at a managerial, classroom and individual level. 'Accelerated learning' is based on the research over the last 15 years on how the brain works: we each have a preferred learning style – a way of learning that suits us best. If you know and use the techniques that match your preferred way of learning, you learn more naturally. Because it is more natural for you, it becomes easier; because it is easier, it is quicker; hence the name – accelerated learning. Both 'emotional literacy' and the 'social and emotional aspects of learning' (SEAL) project promote the fact that, unless the pupil is in an emotionally stable state, no learning will take place. The pupil needs to be able to articulate and discuss his or her emotions – fears, worries, sadness, as well as success, happiness and achievements.

Whatever approach you and your school take, it is important that pupils feel secure in the knowledge that, every time they approach a difficulty, it is a very special time that should be celebrated because new learning is about to take place.

It is vital that each classroom caters for personalised learning, tailoring education to individual needs, interests and aptitudes, to ensure that every pupil achieves and reaches the highest standards possible. It is shaping teaching around the way pupils learn. The learner must be given the navigation skills to cope with the journey. These include:

- the capacity to make informed choices and live with the consequences of those choices;
- the ability to discriminate between relevant and irrelevant information in a variety of contexts;
- the willingness to operate on a daily basis within a moral code;
- everyday problem solving;
- active participation in a number of communities.

And, throughout all the above:

- the ability to feel positive about themselves and others.

Each of the above strategies understands that each child is unique; that a single curriculum is not appropriate for all; and that pupil needs should be taken into account in order to maximise the learning. At a conference of neuroscientists in Granada, Spain, the host (Ball, 2001), in his concluding statement, said:

> We need the science of pedagogy . . . If I can learn in a way that satisfies me, I will learn anything you want me to. But if I cannot learn in a way that is comfortable for me, then I will not learn anything, even if I want to learn it, let alone if you want me to learn it. The 'how' of my learning governs the 'what'. The pedagogy is more important than the curriculum.

CHAPTER SUMMARY

- Effective learning starts with knowledge of the child's needs.
- It is important to let the child have control of his or her own learning.
- Children learn best when they are relaxed and happy, and when they feel included and respected.

REFERENCES

Ball, E. (2001) Closing speech, 43rd International Meeting of the European Tissue Culture Society Cell Interactions and Cellular Complexity, Granada, Spain, 1–3 February.

Binet, A. and Simon, T. (1916/1973) Human Intelligence. Available online at www.indiana.edu/~intell/binet.shtml (accessed 1/3/12).

Clarke, S. (2003) *Enriching Feedback*. London: Hodder & Stoughton.

Clarke, S. (2005) *Formative Assessment in Action: Weaving the elements together*. London: Hodder & Stoughton.

Dommett, E., Devonshire, I. and Churches, R. (2011) *Learning and the Brain Pocketbook*. Winchester: Teachers Pocket Books.

Entwistle, N. (1989) *Styles of Learning and Teaching: An integrated outline of educational psychology for students, teachers and lecturers*. London: David Fulton.

Fleetham, M. (2006) *Multiple Intelligences in Practice*. Stafford: Network Continuum Education.

Franklin Institute (2004) The Brain: Renew Exercise. Available online at www.fi.edu/learn/brain/exercise (accessed 30/9/11).

Ginnis, P. (2002) *The Teacher's Toolkit*. Glasgow: Bell & Bain.

Honey, P. and Mumford, A. (1992) *Manual of Learning Styles*. Maidenhead: Peter Honey.

Jensen, E. (2008) *Brain Based Learning* (2nd edition). Thousand Oaks CA: Corwin Press.

MacBeath, J. and Myers, K. (1999) *Effective School Leaders*. London: Prentice Hall.

Maslow, A. (1943) A theory of human motivation. *The Psychological Review*, 50: 370–96.

Pardoe, D. (2009) *Towards Successful Learning* (2nd edition). Stafford: Network Educational Press.

Royal Society (2011) Brain Waves: Neuroscience: implications for education and lifelong learning. Available online at http://royalsociety.org/policy/projects/brain-waves/education-lifelong-learning (accessed 30/9/11); www.learningandteaching.info/learning/piaget.htm (accessed 30/9/11).

Sousa, D. (2006) *How the Brain Learns* (3rd edition). Thousand Oaks, CA: Corwin Press.

Vygotsky, L.S. (1986) *Thought and Language* (ed. and trans. A. Kozulin). Cambridge, MA: MIT Press.

FURTHER READING

Alfrey, C. (ed.) (2004) *Understanding Children's Learning: A text for teaching assistants*. London: David Fulton.

Assessment Reform Group (2002) *Testing, Motivation and Learning*. Cambridge: University of Cambridge, Faculty of Education.

Black, P., Harrison, C., Lee, C., Marshall, B. and Wiliam, D. (2002) *Working Inside the Black Box*. London: Department of Education and Professional Studies, Kings College.

Bold, C. (2011) *Supporting Learning and Teaching* (2nd edition). London: Routledge.

Carnell, E. and Lodge, C. (2002) *Supporting Effective Learning*. London: Paul Chapman.

De Freitas, S. and Yapp, C. (eds) (2005) *Personalizing Learning in the 21st Century*. Stafford: Network Educational Press.

Goleman, D. (1995*) Emotional Intelligence: Why it can matter more than IQ*. New York: Bantam Dell.

Kerry, T. and Wilding, M. (2004) *Effective Classroom Teacher: Developing the skills you need in today's classroom*. Edinburgh: Pearson Education.

Kyriacou, C. (1997) *Effective Teaching in Schools: Theory and practice*. Cheltenham: Nelson Thornes.

Kyriacou, C. (1998) *Essential Teaching Skills*. Cheltenham: Nelson Thornes.

Prashnig, B. (2006) *Learning Styles in Action*. Stafford: Network Continuum Education.

Smith, A. (1996) *Accelerated Learning in the Classroom*. Stafford: Network Educational Press.

Smith, A. (2002) *The Brain's Behind It*. Stafford: Network Educational Press.

Smith, A. and Call, N. (1999) *The Alps Approach: Accelerated learning in primary schools*. Stafford: Network Educational Press.

Smith, A., Lovatt, M. and Wise, D. (2003) *Accelerated Learning: A user's guide*. Stafford: Network Educational Press.

Watkinson, A. (2006) *Learning and Teaching: The essential guide for higher level teaching assistants*. London: David Fulton.

8 MANAGING CHANGE

Karen Castle and Gillian Goddard

CHAPTER OBJECTIVES

By the end of this chapter you will:

- be able to identify how you will manage changes that take place in your work area;
- be able to identify the implications for managers when implementing change;
- have had the opportunity to reflect on yourself as a change agent;
- have begun to develop some understanding of why change is necessary.

LINKS TO **HLTA** STANDARDS

1. Demonstrate a commitment to collaborative and co-operative working with colleagues.
2. Improve their own knowledge and practice, including responding to advice and feedback.
3. Have sufficient understanding of specialist area(s) of expertise to support the development, learning and progress of children and young people.

Introduction

Change is an integral part of our daily lives and influences many of our decisions and activities, often to the extent that we rarely pause to reflect what effect change is really having on us and on those around us. According to Senge, yesterday's solutions become today's problems (2006, p57), suggesting that change is endemic and unavoidable. The capacity and ability to embrace change and to develop methods to enable us to accept and work with change has become an essential skill, and one that is necessary if we are to function successfully in modern society, and in the workplace.

This chapter will address some of the main issues surrounding change within an organisational context and, in so doing, will focus on change within an educational setting. It will discuss change from two perspectives: first, from the point of view of a manager, implementing change within the organisation; and, second, from the perspective of the individual employee, in identifying strategies to enable them to embrace and manage change from a personal standpoint.

Why do we need change?

Knowledge seems to widen and deepen at an ever-increasing rate, and we, as educational professionals, need to identify some way of managing how we cope with this information and innovation overload. People will form their own ways of dealing with this, which is why the management of change is a diverse and often fragmented area to understand.

In Chapter 2, you were asked to spend some time thinking about how things have changed in relation to the role of the Teaching Assistant (TA), or to discuss change with more experienced colleagues. Now you need not only to revisit these thoughts, but also to think about why the changes occurred.

Some social commentators will argue that we are moving from a modernist world – a world where structure, uniformity and hierarchy exist to provide a framework against which industry operates, and where family and work are separate entities, to a postmodern conception of the world and industry, where we experience fragmentation, alienation and uncertainty – a world in which work life and family life 'mesh' together and employers and organisations exercise more flexible, collegial and democratic ways of operation. Social theorists have suggested that postmodern society today is unpredictable and constantly changing, and that it can be volatile and chaotic. Morrison (1998) identified that many organisations employ managers whose roles increasingly involve managing this unpredictability, volatility and change. His name for this type of manager is 'impression manager'.

It would seem that change is inherent in a postmodern society, due to fragmentation and ever-changing bureaucratisation. However, despite this, many organisations are still clutching on to what is left of a modernistic framework and are, therefore, operating against the old and out-of-date 'factory' model. Hargreaves (1994) argues that most large educational institutions are typical of modernist organisations. Many operate a hierarchical structure; for example, with decision making being the sole preserve of the head teacher, and with a hierarchical approach to new innovations and ideas, using the National Curriculum as a framework against which to develop and deliver teaching could be perceived as a prescriptive format that has served to remove the autonomy of the teacher, in particular in terms of dictating the pedagogical element of teaching. It could be suggested, therefore, that schools need to change and adapt in order to become more flexible in the ways in which they meet the needs of pupils, students and staff, and this adaptation and flexibility could be viewed as precursors to becoming postmodern institutions. Furthermore, schools could become independently run units, dominated less by local authority bureaucracy and developing a more flexible approach to teaching and learning, maybe involving the local community. If the strategic and organisational aspect of the school is to change, the roles of the staff within the organisation will also need to undergo change.

For the purposes of this chapter, it is necessary to highlight, in particular, the role of the TA. It would seem that the role has changed dramatically over recent years, to encompass more responsibility and a greater range of tasks:

> *The teaching assistant now has a stronger role in the educational process as well as the more traditional roles of childcare, preparation, classroom organisation and pastoral care . . . teaching assistants need to be more flexible and innovative in order to meet the varied needs of their job. In successful schools, the role of the teaching assistant has developed to meet the needs*

of a more complex and demanding curriculum, larger teaching groups, a perceived increase in SEN pupils and increase in the level of formal assessment.

(Kay, 2005, p11)

Training and professional development for TAs has increased and become more focused in order to meet the demands of the new role. Higher Level Teaching Assistant (HLTA) status is awarded to those TAs who have successfully completed the HLTA training programme; similarly, foundation degrees provide a qualification structure for TAs to further their skills and career. It would, therefore, appear that significant changes have taken, and are taking place in the field of education, and it seems pertinent to suggest that those working within this environment need to identify and manage these changes successfully if the arena of education is to flourish.

CASE STUDY 1

Blackwater Secondary School is a large inner-city comprehensive school that has just been put into special measures following a less than satisfactory Ofsted inspection. One of the main areas of concern for the Ofsted inspectors was the apparent inflexibility of the organisation in responding to change. It was identified that the community within which the school is situated had changed considerably as there had been a high percentage of foreign families moving into the area. The increase in people who had English as a second language had impacted significantly on the community in general; however, the school had not identified with these changes, and was found to be lacking in several areas.

REFLECTIVE TASK

Give some consideration to case study 1 and reflect on the situation.

- What changes do you think the school could make in order to address the issue of foreign pupils?
- What impact would this have on staff at the school?
- What impact would this have on the pupils?
- What impact would this have on the community?

PRACTICAL TASK

Find out what the policy is in your school for pupils who have English as an additional language.

- Where is the policy kept?
- Is it easily accessible?

External influences

It has been argued that organisations need to change so that they are competitive in the marketplace. Most organisations operate against some degree of competition; retail outlets have historically needed to undercut or outsell their nearest competitor, or face a decline in profits. Service providers have traditionally experienced a less competitive approach, but this would appear to be changing. Educational institutions are often in competition with neighbouring training providers, whether independent, public or private sector, as the marketplace adapts to the changes in demand for the products or services. Businesses merge and, therefore, need to absorb change to enable the merger to be effective. Press publications routinely carry stories of business mergers or 'buy out' deals, often resulting in an insecure workforce and anxieties within the community. As a result of the falling pupil numbers in some schools, the education sector, from time to time, experiences school mergers. It follows, therefore, that staff within these schools will be feeling insecure as they apply for a limited number of posts within the newly merged school. Enabling these staff to positively embrace this type of change is extremely challenging. Parents and other stakeholders could also be anxious about mergers, particularly if the mergers result in children needing to travel further afield.

Political changes and initiatives from government at a national level will impact on organisations at a local level. External influences such as these are often unpredictable and therefore less able to be predetermined, which could result in managers and leaders being less able to demonstrate a proactive approach to change and, in some cases, appearing distant or remote from the change. It is very difficult for managers to plan for change that is, in some cases, unpredictable. However, Handy (2001) identified that managers need to keep a keen eye on the future and make changes appropriate to their judgement of what the future might hold. He went on to argue that the time at which they make a change is paramount to the change being effective. For example, if a manager left implementing change too late, they would be seen as a manager who led their workforce into decline; if they implemented the change too early, the perceived premature nature of the change may serve to convince the workforce that it is unnecessary.

CASE STUDY 2

The village of Cauldside has been investigating the possibility of having an 'out of school club'. The community want a safe and secure area for schoolchildren to access before and after their school day. At a recent village committee, it was decided to approach the three schools within the area, to ask if they would be interested in hosting such a club. Funding for this project will be met by the local government who have secured funding for five years. It is felt that this project will provide a degree of kudos for the school that is successful in its bid to host the club.

REFLECTIVE TASK

What could the schools in case study 2 do in order to ensure that they have a good chance of success in the bid to host the out of school club?

- What could be the schools' strengths?
- What could be the schools' weak areas?
- What changes would need to be considered by the heads of the schools?

REFLECTIVE TASK

- What external influences have impacted on the changes to your organisation? Give some thought to how these changes have been identified and what source they came from.
- What external influences have impacted on the changes to your own role? How has the role of the TA responded to these external influences?

PRACTICAL TASK

Select five colleagues and discuss their views of how external influences have impacted on their role. Do they feel this has been a positive or negative impact? Find out why.

Internal influences

Organisations need to be able to react to changes relating to their own strategies, often in response to a revision of goals or targets, or in response to making better use of resources. One of the most influential internal causes for innovation is the need for the organisation to change in order to improve standards. For example, a school may need to implement different strategies in order to respond to a recent OFSTED report. Performance management targets could impact on the way in which the staff appraisal process needs to change. Head teachers will need to implement changes to the way in which the school operates and, in so doing, may introduce new methods of working for the staff or new resources. Fullan (2007) reported that, in order to reform, schools need to do more that just put into place a new policy. Rather, they need to change the culture of the classroom and the organisation. Losing members of staff and gaining new members effects a change to the organisation, and this is happening every day in schools up and down the country. The existing staff will need to get used to the new dynamic that the staff changes will inevitably bring, and this means forging new relationships and interactions.

CASE STUDY 3

Primrose Dale is a large primary school that has recently been formed as a result of the merger of two small rural primary schools. The head teacher has recently held a consultative meeting with staff to discuss how they view the future of the school. One of the main issues discussed was the changing role of the TAs. It would seem that, prior to the merger, the TAs at both of the smaller schools were responsible for such duties as assisting the teacher with tasks such as preparing art and craft resources, helping with photocopying, supporting some of the children in lessons with reading and writing, helping to prepare lessons and looking after children who were ill. The head teacher now wanted the TAs to change their role, and take part in professional development activities that would enable them to have greater responsibility and more accountability.

REFLECTIVE TASK

Reflecting on case study 3, how would you feel if you were a TA at Primrose Dale? How would you feel about taking on more responsibility and participating in professional development? Why would you feel this way?

PRACTICAL TASK
Discuss with your head teacher, or deputy head, the organisational policy for implementing change. Find out how internal change is disseminated to staff.

Change in an educational context

It would seem pertinent, therefore, to argue that organisations need to change in response to a variety of influences. Educational settings, being organisations themselves, also need to change. During the 1980s and 1990s, changes to educational policy in terms of the devolution of budget control and marketisation forced the management of schools to become more focused on a business model. In conflict with this, Wilby (1997) argued that education should not initiate business practices, as business is seen as less than moral. It is often undemocratic and obsessed with image as opposed to substance, being driven by profit. There are many and varied arguments comparing the business and educational models, and this chapter will not address these in any depth. However, it is apt to appreciate that these arguments exist and are often the catalyst for educational change today.

It is probably fair to say that education has changed considerably over the past few years, both from a curriculum point of view and from a strategic perspective. Watkinson (2003) has identified that the practices of the past and people's attitudes to work will need to change in order to adapt to future developments. She has found that the new role of the TA will require them to work much more closely with teaching staff.

There has been a dramatic expansion of support staff in schools growing, for example, from a ratio of one TA for every 6.6 teachers in 1997 to one TA to 2.5 teachers by 2007 (DfES, 2007, cited in Edmund and Price, 2009) The government had proposed that the increasing demands on classroom teachers will be alleviated by the TA, in terms of HLTAs covering classes in order that teachers can be released to perform other tasks (DfES, 2003). It further suggests that the classroom is no longer the sole preserve of the teacher (DfES, 2003, p6).

CASE STUDY 4
Dunromin Secondary School has just received training school status, and as a result will be the central school for continuing professional development (CPD) and training for education professionals within the area. It will also be able to offer the graduate teaching programme. The change in status of the school has led to the head teacher making changes to the way in which the school approaches CPD. This, in turn, has led to several HLTAs taking lessons and performing many of the tasks that were once the domain of the teacher. This has been received well by the majority of staff, but there are a few staff who have reacted quite negatively towards the change to the role of the TAs.

REFLECTIVE TASK
• In case study 4, how could the TAs respond to the staff who view the change in a negative way? What are the implications for the school in this case?

- There has been a large increase in numbers of school support staff over the last ten years. Why do you think this is?
- Reflecting on your own work area, what implications has this increase had on the way in which the organisation operates?

PRACTICAL TASK

Have a look on the website www.dcsf.gov.uk and try to identify some of the more recent changes that might affect the school where you work.

Change from the point of view of the individual

People are often called upon to adapt to new ways of working, learn new tasks and embrace new technology. Once the change is implemented they must learn to cope with the impact the change has on them and on their role. It is important to realise that people will need time to adapt to new systems and processes. People generally develop their performance gradually and over different periods of time depending on the individual. Carnall (2007) has argued that significant organisational changes can create a decline in self-esteem. If we understand that workers in any organisation become more confident in their role as they build up a wealth of understanding and knowledge developed from their experience and skills, we can see that their confidence could easily become disrupted if they need to learn new skills or operate under unfamiliar regimes. I would argue strongly that people need support and guidance though the change, and that they need to feel safe through the process of change, not just at the implementation stage, but consistently throughout. Furthermore, people need to know how they have managed the change; they need to receive objective feedback on their actions.

Peer support can offer workers the opportunity to discuss problems and anxieties in a non-threatening environment, maybe by introducing humour in order to lighten the situation and to help in discovering coping mechanisms. Many workers will be terrified of making a mistake or showing themselves up in front of colleagues, particularly when they have previously been able to carry out tasks almost as second nature.

Coping with change requires the individuals to identify coping strategies. Prior to this, the individuals need to be able to understand themselves and, in so doing, to reflect on such issues as: How will I be affected by this change? Am I going to be able to accept the change? What is the worst thing that can happen to me? What will be of most benefit to me?

If the change involves a different job role, the individuals need to identify what skills and abilities are needed for the new role and if they are able to develop their own skills. They may need help in doing this, but they may not always acknowledge their need for help.

Where the change involves working with different people, the individuals need to reflect on their own communication and interaction skills – do these need to be developed? Has this situation happened before and, if so, how did individuals react in that situation? Very often we don't fully appreciate the skills that we have used in previous situations and that are transferable to current events.

CASE STUDY 5

Reuben has been a TA for five years. He has just begun to study for a foundation degree in supporting teaching and learning and has been supported in his CPD by the head teacher. Reuben has identified that he would like to take part in any of the school's developmental activities and has been pro-active in identifying such opportunities. The head teacher therefore asked Reuben if he would take a leading role in introducing the interactive whiteboard to the classroom. The head wants to put whiteboards in every classroom and has realised the need for staff to be trained in the use of the board. The head has informed Reuben that he will attend a training course and then return to the school to train the other members of staff in the use of the board.

Reuben, however, is very anxious about training the other staff, as he feels somewhat intimidated by some of the other teachers. He is happy with the fact that he will learn about the new innovation, but is less confident with his skills as a trainer.

REFLECTIVE TASK

- Reflecting on case study 5, what would you do if you were in Reuben's position, and why would you act in such a way?
- How differently could the head teacher have approached this?
- Think about how you respond to change in different situations. Do you, for example, react differently to change at work than you would to a change in your social arrangements?
- How would you respond to a change to your working hours – a situation that may impact on your home life and family? Why would you react in this way?

PRACTICAL TASK

Select a group of colleagues and social contacts and find out from them how they personally respond to change. Design a small questionnaire and ask each of them to complete it. Once you have received their responses, give some thought to what they have said.

Resistance to change

There appears to be a deep-seated belief that change is difficult; that it is something to be feared, or to feel threatened by. Some authors argue that people are conditioned to be resistant to change. But why might this be the case? Carnall (2007) argues that resistance to change is derived from the mismanagement of the introduction of change. If people understand what is expected of them, what the outcomes of the change are likely to be and the impact on them as individuals, it seems that resistance to change may be lessened. An organisation in which shared goals are not experienced could be at a disadvantage in terms of achieving a workforce that embraces change. For example, the senior management goals might be to increase the number of pupils achieving a pass at a certain level, whereas the goal of a certain class teacher may be focused on improving literacy. Some people may be resistant to change as they have had previous bad experiences of having to deal with it, or maybe they resist change as it will impact on their family. For example, if a manager wants to implement an extended day, the hours that workers will need to work will change. This could impact on family and social life.

In a recent survey carried out by the author into the way in which CPD has been introduced to school staff, the following responses were among the data received:

- 'Why do I need to start doing this? It won't make a difference to my salary, won't guarantee job security.'
- 'I've been teaching this way for 12 years. I have not had a poor appraisal, so why should I change now?'
- 'If it isn't one thing it's another. Why can't we just leave things alone, and allow ourselves to catch up to where we need to be? It seems to me that you are introducing change for change's sake, particularly when we are so busy just trying to maintain the status quo.'

It seems that, faced with change, people find real value and pertinence in their present situation. Sayings such as: 'If it isn't broken, why fix it?' and 'Don't change a winning team' often resonate from staff rooms.

CASE STUDY 6

Bella Cairn is 55 and has been a TA for 30 years. She is well liked by the children and staff and is respected within the village community in which the school is situated. Bella decided not to take part in any professional development as she felt that, as she had been working in school for so long, she didn't really need to learn anything more. She had never had a bad report from the head and had constantly been told that she does a good job. Bella had always found it difficult to understand why other TAs would want to take part in any training courses or programmes, and had often told them that they were wasting their time and what they were learning would change anyway.

REFLECTIVE TASK

Think about case study 6 and reflect on why Bella might be feeling this way.

- Why would she pass her negative feelings on to other TAs who could quite easily be influenced by her?
- How might the other TAs respond to her?

Now imagine that you are a TA working with Bella and you have just begun to study for a foundation degree. How might you feel as a result of what Bella is saying and how would you handle this situation?

PRACTICAL TASK

How can you show colleagues that you can support them with their learning and encourage them to take part in professional development? What would your actions be if you were asked to support a more junior member of staff?

Change from the point of view of a manager

The ways in which the school is managed, in terms of the style of leadership and management demonstrated by the head teacher and deputies, affect and impact on the way in which change is received by the workforce within the school. People need to feel that change in necessary, and that it isn't implemented for the sake of it. Workers often feel that change is made by managers purely to justify their own positions within the hierarchy of the organisation, or as a 'knee jerk' reaction to internal or external influences. Managers and leaders responsible for change need to identify clear and effective communication systems within the organisation. If there are poor communication channels, or if managers are 'out of reach' of the workforce, anxieties and concerns that the workforce have will not be aired and are, therefore, likely to become significant issues as time progresses. Workers need to feel that they are important to the overall effectiveness and success of the organisation. Only when workers feel safe and unthreatened are they likely to embrace change in a manner that is appropriate to the organisation as a whole. Similarly, the workforce needs to feel supported through the change process. As mentioned earlier, workers need time to adjust to the change, and managers will benefit from giving time to their staff, and supporting them through the change.

Take some time to consider the scenario in case study 7, which is taken from a true situation.

CASE STUDY 7

A special needs unit within a large secondary school had been earmarked for closure. The unit was managed by a special educational needs co-ordinator (SENCO), supported by teachers and TAs. The staff had been told that the unit was probably going to have to restructure and that this would impact on their roles in the future. They were informed that it was unlikely that they would be made redundant, as they would be needed to support the children with special needs in the respective classes. The SENCO had voiced the concerns of the staff on several occasions, the unit staff were concerned that their jobs were no longer secure and several of the teachers from other areas were concerned that the children with special needs would have a detrimental impact on their classes. One Monday morning, the unit staff opened their e-mails to learn that the unit would close at the end of that term (in approximately four weeks' time). The head teacher had informed them by e-mail of this and had asked them, if they had any questions or queries, to make an appointment with him the following day.

This situation led to the SENCO resigning and several of the other staff feeling aggrieved and undervalued.

REFLECTIVE TASK

How could the situation in case study 7 have been handled differently? How would you have felt if you were one of the TAs in the unit?

PRACTICAL TASK

Talk to the head teacher or deputy head teacher at your school and ask them to discuss with you their view of managing change. How would they implement change to the school workforce? What do they think are the most important things to remember?

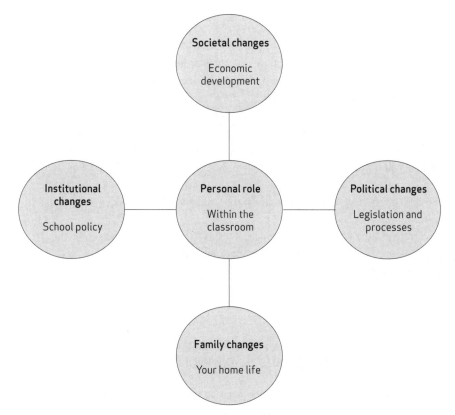

Figure 8.1: A metaphor for change (adapted from Parker et al., 2009)

REFLECTIVE TASK
Have a look at Figure 8.1 and place yourself in the middle circle. How are you affected by the three driving forces for change?

PRACTICAL TASK
Think about a recent change that you were involved with:

- in your school;
- in your classroom;
- with a pupil.

Now answer the following.

- Who or what generated the change?
- How was the change implemented?
- Who supported the change? And how?
- Who resisted the change? And how?
- What was your role in the change?
- How did the situation conclude?
- What have you learned from this about change and how to handle it?

CHAPTER SUMMARY

- The role of the TA has changed significantly over the past few years.
- There are many different catalysts for change and these impact on the individual and the organisation in different and diverse ways.
- Managing change can be approached from different angles: for example, from the point of view of the manager or change agent implementing the change, and from the point of view of the individual in managing the way that change impacts on them and their role.
- Some people will support and react positively to change, while others will resist or reject change.
- If change is to be effective, it must influence and be influenced by the values of the staff and the organisation.
- Change cannot be hurried or rushed through. It needs to take time, to give people the opportunity to digest the change and seek support and guidance as necessary.
- Change is too important to leave to the experts.

REFERENCES

Carnall, C. (2007) *Managing Change in Organisations* (5th edition). London: Prentice Hall.

Department for Education and Skills (DfES) (2003) *Developing the Role of School Support Staff*. London: DfES.

Department for Education and Skills (DfES) (2007) *School Workforce in England (including pupil: teacher ratios and pupil: adult ratios)*, January (revised). London: DfES.

Edmund, N. and Price, M. (2009) Workforce re-modelling and pastoral care in schools: a diversification of roles or a de-professionalisation of functions?, *Pastoral Care in Education*, 27(4): 301–11

Fullan, M. (2007) *The New Meaning of Educational Change* (4th edition). London: Routledge.

Handy, C. (2001) *The Empty Raincoat*. London: Random House.

Hargreaves, A. (1994) *Changing Teachers, Changing Times*. London: Teachers College Press.

Kay, J. (2005) *Teaching Assistant's Handbook (Primary Edition)*. London: Continuum.

Morrison, K. (1998) *Management Theories for Educational Change*. London: Paul Chapman.

Senge, P. (2006) *The Fifth Discipline* (2nd edition). New York: Random House.

Parker, M., Lee, C., Gunn, S., Heardman, K., Hincks-Knight, R., Pittman, M. and Townsend, M. (2009) *A Toolkit for the Effective Teaching Assistant* (2nd edition). London: Sage.

Watkinson, A. (2003) *The Essential Guide for Competent Teaching Assistants: Meeting the national occupational standards at level 2*. London: David Fulton.

Wilby, P. (1997) Stopping the clocks on inequality will not stem it. *Times Educational Supplement*, 28 November.

FURTHER READING

Handy, C. (1993) *Understanding Organisations*. London: Penguin.

Whitaker, P. (1999) *Managing Schools*. Oxford: Butterworth.

9 TEACHING READING USING SYNTHETIC PHONICS

Karen Boardman

CHAPTER OBJECTIVES

By the end of this chapter you will have:

- understood the current practice and theories linked to the development of reading in children;

- understood the value of synthetic phonics programmes for young children;

- identified and reflect on strategies to support pupils who are exhibiting reading difficulties.

LINKS TO **HLTA** STANDARDS

1. Have high expectations of children and young people with a commitment to helping them fulfil their potential.

2. Improve their own knowledge and practice, including responding to advice and feedback.

3. Understand the key factors that affect children's and young people's learning and progress.

4. Know how to contribute to effective personalised provision by taking practical account of diversity.

5. Have sufficient understanding of their area(s) of expertise to support the development, learning and progress of children and young people.

6. Understand the objectives, content and intended outcomes for the learning activities in which they are involved.

7. Devise clearly structured activities that interest and motivate learners and advance their learning.

8. Contribute to the selection and preparation of resources suitable for children's and young people's interests and abilities.

Introduction

This chapter examines current practice and theories linked to the development of reading in children. It will discuss the rationale and the value of synthetic phonics programmes, and will enable you to identify and select effective support strategies for those pupils experiencing reading difficulties.

The development of reading

Learning to read is a complex matter. Reading is one of the most important skills to learn in life. It enables us to find out new snippets of information and have a breadth of endless opportunities. Reading books and stories together is one of the fundamental cornerstones of reading. Access to books and a wide variety of reading material, especially good quality, is essential if children are to build a good foundation of reading in their early years (Nutbrown, 2006). Early Years is a crucial stage in establishing enthusiasm for books and reading. Lockwood (2008: 49) comments that *positive attitudes created at the early years stage can set the pattern for life.*

It is widely agreed that interesting children in literacy through a variety of fun activities from the Early Years is significant. *The Practice Guidance for the Early Years Foundation Stage* (May, 2008) promotes effective practice from birth, *tell as well as read stories with young babies and let children handle books and draw their attention to pictures* as early as 8 months old (DCSF, 2008, p55). Early Years Practitioners are advised to plan environments that are rich in signs, symbols, notices, rhymes, books, pictures, music and songs that consider the differing intersects, home backgrounds and various cultures of young children from birth to five (DCFS, 2008).

Children learn and develop as individuals. Goouch and Lambirth (2011, p6) state that *children are different and may learn differently* and this applies equally to their skills in learning to read. In the early phases of learning and development, children will act out reading behaviour by holding the book, looking at the words and pictures and turning pages. They will later begin to understand that the words carry meaning and point to familiar words. As they progress further they will:

- retell and read familiar texts;
- attempt unfamiliar texts by reading word for word;
- start sounding out and using picture cues to help them.

Children will then begin to employ various strategies to enable them to read different types of texts before finally becoming independent readers, by which time strategies are applied automatically.

According to Browne, the foundation for reading is traditionally established between the ages of four and eight, but the process begins before this and continues after it (2002, p26). She goes on to say:

> Learning to read does not necessarily begin at 4, neither does it end at 8. All children need supported experiences with books and practice at reading a variety of texts before they are fluent.
> (Browne, 2002, p27)

This is also iterated in Early Years Foundation Stage by the DCSF, who say that at 22–36 months children will be looking at picture books and listening to stories, being important steps in literacy (DCSF, 2008).

> *Before they come to school, children will have been exposed to a great deal of print in many contexts, from reading stories in their homes, to seeing signs on shops and being able to spot their favourite brand of breakfast cereal. It is, therefore, important to start with what the child already knows. Children need to understand that reading is enjoyable and informative and relevant to their present lives.*
>
> (DCSF, 2008, p38)

Smith (1976) and Nutbrown (2006) suggest that reading begins the moment young children become aware of environmental print. *Environmental print can stimulate talk about literacy as children ask questions such as 'What does that say?' It also prompts children, at times, to pick out and identify from signs some letters that are familiar to them, perhaps in their own name* (Nutbrown, 2006, p44). Early Years Practitioners can support children in their pre-reading skills by focusing on meaningful print such as the child's name, words on a cereal packet or a book title, in order to discuss similarities and differences between symbols as part of everyday continuous provision and practice.

So how can we, as practitioners, help support and develop the reading skills of the children we are working with? Consider the following.

There are several theories about the reading process which can usually be grouped into two different 'trains of thought'.

The 'top down' theories involve the reader using descriptive clues from graphic information and context to anticipate meaning (Reid, 2003).

The 'bottom-up' theories believe that the key to a child's reading is learning to decode words by being taught letter-sound correspondences, which in turn lead to automaticity to whole word recognition.

Are there any common links between the above theories?

Snowling and Hulme (2010) suggest that reading develops through stages and that the stages are often interchangeable through the theories. Vellutino et al. (2004) discuss that the process of reading involves fluent word identification and comprehension of text. For children to acquire phonemic awareness, direct teaching is necessary (Goswami, 2008).

The current teaching of reading in schools has encompassed this 'bottom-up' theory by implementing the use of systematic synthetic phonics and the introduction of the *Letters and Sounds* (DfES, 2007) programme in 2007 as part of the National Primary Strategy.

The publication of Jim Rose's *Independent Review of the Teaching of Early Reading* in 2006, and The Primary National Strategy's, *Primary Framework for Literacy and Mathematics* in 2006 clearly advocated the Simple View of Reading as a model for how children learn to read. The Rose Review (Rose, 2006) concluded that the systematic synthetic phonics approach was the most effective method to teach young children to learn to read. The recommendations from the Rose Review (Rose, 2006) led to the publication of *Letters and Sounds* (DfES, 2007), replacing the earlier *Progression in Phonics* (DfEE, 1999) and *Playing with Sounds*, which used an analytical phonics approach to reading.

Rose (2006) promotes the link between decoding and meaning as essential for text comprehension . . . *words must be decoded if readers are to make sense of the text.* (2006, p5). He strongly advocated that the word recognition component of reading should include high quality phonics work and this should be taught with systematic synthetic phonics.

The Primary Framework for Literacy and Numeracy /Primary National Strategy report advocates a:

> *systematic programme of high-quality phonic work, time limited and reinforced throughout the curriculum with careful assessment and monitoring of children's progress as they move from learning to read towards reading to learn, engaging with diverse texts for purpose and pleasure.*
>
> (DfES, 2006, p7)

REFLECTIVE TASK

What do you think about all these statements? What teaching methods and strategies are you aware of or do you employ in your setting to help children to learn to read? How do you ensure that you start with what the child already knows?

In the Foundation Stage, effective teaching requires practitioners to demonstrate the use of language for reading and writing . . . through telling stories and sharing books in a clear and lively way that motivates children (DfEE, 2000, p46). By the end of the Foundation Stage, children are expected to be able to read a range of familiar and common words and simple sentences independently (DCSF, 2008). The 'prime approach' used to achieve this is phonics.

By the end of Year 2, the DCSF believe that the development of children's phonic knowledge, skills and understanding is time limited and the majority of children will usually achieve the learning objectives . . . by the end of Key Stage 1 (DCSF, 2008). The emphasis then switches from word recognition to language comprehension and, by the end of Key Stage 2, the objective is for children to read extensively and discuss their reading with others.

As children progress through Key Stages 3 and 4, the new Secondary Framework for English places the emphasis on 'reading for meaning', using a range of strategies and the ability to analyse, compare and respond to layers of meaning, subtlety and allusion in texts and contrast texts (DCSF, 2008, p13).

The question that still remains is how do we teach reading?

You may be surprised to learn that the debate between 'whole word' teaching methods and phonics is not new. In America in the late 1800s, a phonic series of books known as McGuffy Readers was very popular (Snowling and Hulme, 2007). These books reviewed previously taught letter sounds and then introduced new ones. Those of you familiar with Jolly Phonics may recall the action for 'h' – 'Hold hand in front of mouth panting as if you are out of breath and say h, h, h' (Lloyd and Wernham, 2005). These methods however were not embraced by all. Adams (1990) argued that the phonics approach undermined the young readers' ability to understand what they are actually reading.

The debate continued with the whole word approach dominating the scene in the early to mid twentieth century, with the emphasis on authentic children's literature and the minimising of phonics or phonics-influenced texts (Snowling and Hulme 2007, p507). The whole language approach to reading also developed due to a changing child-centred educational philosophy, thus influenced by the work of Piaget (Johnston and Watson 2007).

PRACTICAL TASK

Take a look at the range of books and other materials used in your setting to teach reading. Are you able to identify a phonic or whole word approach? What about the stories, illustrations and styles? Do they match the levels of interest for the children you work with? Make a short list using the table below (the first one has been completed for you as an example).

Title	Scheme/ Author	Whole word/ Phonic	Age band (if given or best guess)	Readability
Cat in a bag	Oxford Reading Tree	Phonic and high-frequency words	4–5	Lots of colourful pictures to add interest for this age group

We must also think carefully about ourselves as role models when it comes to developing an interest in reading for the children in our schools. Do they see us reading for purpose and enjoyment? Or are we too focused on the mechanics of reading?

Consider this statement from Hall (2003):

> *the way they are taught reading conveys to them powerful messages about what reading is and what it is good for.*

(2003: 194)

Cremin et al. (2008) argue that:

> *professionals need to pay more attention to children's attitudes, their preferences, pleasures and perceptions of themselves as readers in order to help ensure that they develop as readers who not only can, but do choose to read for pleasure and for life.*

(2008, p166)

How do you 'pay attention' to young children's reading for pleasure? Is reading a pleasurable experience in your setting or a mechanical, structured approach?

Is reading a continued focus in secondary settings?

Introduction to synthetic phonics programmes

Johnston and Watson (2007) state that phonic approaches to teaching reading in schools capitalise on the fact that our spelling system is alphabetic. In languages over the world, children learn to identify syllables first and then become aware of the onset-rime division (Port, 2006). Dombey (2009) argues that it is not easy for children to learn to recognise individual phonemes in English. English uses an alphabetical writing system, in which graphemes (letters and groups of letters) represent phonemes (speech sounds). It is, however, extremely important that everyone involved in teaching children to read uses consistent terminology and reinforces the correct understanding (Hickey, 2009).

Does this mean that once you have mastered the English alphabetic code, you can read any and all words?

What is synthetic phonics?

Synthetic phonics is the recommended approach to teaching phonics to children. Synthetic phonics teaches children to 'build up' words through sounding them out one grapheme at a time. It is seen to be particularly appropriate for children beginning schooling, where they are yet unable to read and nearly all written words are unfamiliar to them. The term 'synthetic' in synthetic phonics means to 'synthesise' (i.e. put together or build up) pronunciations for unfamiliar written words by translating letters into sounds and blending the sounds together ('blending' = 'synthesising'). Synthetic phonics is also used in Germany and Austria, and is generally taught before children are introduced to books or reading.

In a UK version of synthetic phonics, i.e. *Hickey Multi-Sensory Language Course* (Augur and Briggs, 1992), the first block of letter sounds is 's', 'a', 't', 'i', 'p' and 'n', which make up more three-letter words than any other six letters. An example of this is that, when the children have learnt these letter sounds, they are able to blend these letters into words such as 'at', 'pat', 'tap', 'sat', 'pin', 'tin', and so on.

In 1998, Johnston and Watson undertook a study in Clackmannanshire to examine the effects of three types of phonics programmes on the reading and spelling of children in their first year of school (Primary 1 in Scotland, equivalent to Reception in England). The programmes lasted for 16 weeks, for 20 minutes a day. At the end of the study, the findings showed that those children who were taught the synthetic phonics programme were seven months ahead for their age in word reading and spelling. They also found that children who had been taught by the synthetic phonics method not only read and spelt very much above the average for their age, but that these skills increased year after year (Johnston and Watson, 2005).

Rose Review (2006)

Research into the best way to teach reading was undertaken by Jim Rose on behalf of the Department for Education and Skills (DfES, 2006). His final report was published in 2006, giving guidance on future policy on the teaching of reading in England. This study arose from many recommendations around the National Literacy Strategy (NLS) and what methods schools used to teach reading (House of Commons Education and Skills Committee, 2004). The Clackmannanshire study, as discussed previously, was also highlighted in one of the recommendations made by the House of Commons Education and Skills Committee, as one of the reasons why a comparative study into the teaching of synthetic phonics with the NLS should be completed.

As a result of the recommendations, the DfES asked Jim Rose and a panel of advisers to:

examine current evidence about practices for teaching children to read to ensure the Strategy can continue to provide the most effective support assuring children's progression in reading.

(DfES, 2006)

Below are highlighted the five aspects the Rose Review committee examined, together with their findings of these, which were published in the final report (adapted from Lewis and Ellis, 2006).

1 What best practice should be expected in the teaching of the early reading and synthetic phonics.
   - Priority and clear guidance should be given to developing children's speaking and listening skills.
   - High-quality, systematic phonic work as defined by the review should be taught discretely as the prime approach in learning to decode (to read) and encode (to write/spell) print.
   - Phonic work should be set within a broad and rich language curriculum.
   - The Primary National Strategy should continue to exemplify the kind of teaching all children should experience (quality-first teaching).

2 How this relates to the development of the Early Years Foundation Stage and the development and renewal of the National Literacy Strategy Framework for Teaching.
   - For most children, high-quality, systematic phonic work should start by the age of five. This should be multi-sensory.
   - The Searchlight model of reading should be reconstructed.
   - The Early Years Foundation Stage and the renewed literacy framework must be compatible with each other, and give guidance on the continuity and progression in phonic work.

3 What range of provision best supports children with significant literacy difficulties and enables them to catch up with their peers, and the relationship of such targeted intervention programmes with synthetic phonic teaching.
   • High-quality phonic work should be a priority within normal classroom teaching.
   • Additional support should be compatible within mainstream practice.
   • Interventions should be matched to the different types of special educational needs.

4 How leadership and management in schools can support the teaching of reading, as well as practitioners' subject knowledge.
   • Leaders should make sure that phonic work is given appropriate priority in the teaching of beginner readers.
   • At least one member of staff should be able to lead on literacy, especially phonic work.

5 Leaders should monitor the quality and consistency of phonic work and give staff feedback.
   • The value for money or cost-effectiveness of the range of approaches the review considers.
   • Develop a series of additional training of teachers with in-service training and with LA.
   • Increase professional development opportunities to also increase teacher, trainee and TA knowledge about early reading, particularly phonics.

> **REFLECTIVE TASK**
> Using the list above containing the recommendations, how have these been implemented in your school setting? What impact have they made?

Letters and Sounds

The Primary National Strategy programme *Letters and Sounds* (DfES, 2007) is a synthetic phonics programme that replaces both the *Progression in Phonics* and *Playing with Sounds*. The *Letters and Sounds* programme does not build on these previous documents as it is a different type of phonics approach.

Letters and Sounds adopts the 'Simple View of Reading' outlined in the *Rose Review* (DfES, 2006), identifying two dimensions of reading – 'word recognition' and 'language comprehension'.

The *Letters and Sounds* programme offers clear guidance on how to teach letters with a multi-sensory approach. As children learn the letter sound, they learn to form the letter in sand, on a whiteboard and also in the air. *Letters and Sounds* also advocates children using magnetic letters and boards alongside the teacher's whiteboard. Learning the visual shape, the sound and the movement of the letter all at the same time will help the children to consolidate their learning of letters and sounds.

The Simple View of Reading (SVR) model

The Simple View of Reading (SVR) is a model of the process of learning to read (Dombey 2009). The 'Simple View' shows that, to become proficient readers and writers, children must develop both word recognition and language comprehension. This programme focuses on securing word recognition skills as these are essential for children to decode (read) and encode (spell) words accurately. This process then concentrates on comprehending and composing text (DfES, 2007). The *Letters and Sounds: Notes of guidance* (2007) state specifically that children should not use unreliable strategies for attempting unfamiliar words, such as looking at pictures of looking at the first sound and then guessing the word. We need to be clear that the 'Simple View of Reading' model replaces the previous 'Searchlights' model. For beginning readers, priority should be given to securing word recognition knowledge and skills. This means that 'high-quality phonic work', as defined in the *Rose Review* (2006), should be the prime approach used when teaching beginninners to read and spell (DCFS, 2008).

REFLECTIVE TASK

Consider the *Notes of Guidance* statement above. How does this fit in with your settings reading scheme?

The *Letters and Sounds* programme enables children to see the relationship between reading and spelling, with the teaching of one reinforcing the understanding of the other. It is structured into six phases: *Letters and Sounds: Notes of guidance* makes it clear that the boundaries between each phase are not fixed. Detailed below is a brief summary of each phase.

Phase 1

Phase 1 is not part of the phonic teaching programme but prepares children for phonic work. This phase is to be carried out in the Early Years Foundation Stage where speaking and listening skills are developed. Activities are included to develop oral blending and segmenting of the sounds of spoken words.

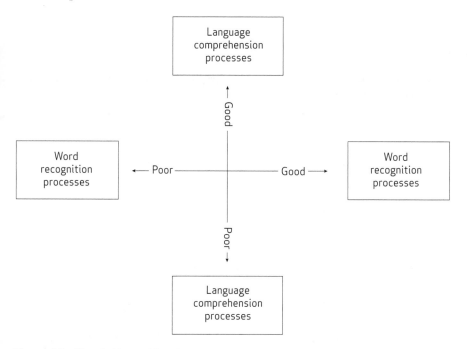

Figure 9.1: Simple View of Reading model

Phase 2

Phonic teaching starts to take place in this phase, where 19 letters of the alphabet are taught. Pupils learn the visual appearance, the sounds and the formation of these letters. The main focus in this stage is that children understand that blending and segmenting are reversible processes.

Pupils use sounding and blending for reading, converting the letters into sounds, for example the word 'sat'. The child knows the letter sounds 's', 'a' and 't', so by saying them from left to right and then blending them together, the child identifies the word as 'sat'.

Children will be able to segment for spelling, where the child hears the word and then breaks it down into its component sounds. For example, when learning to read the word 'tap', the child will take each sound in turn and take the relevant letter each time to form the word: 't', 'a' and 'p'. The child will blend the letter sounds together to check they have the correct spelling and word.

By doing these processes, children will soon be able to read and spell simple Vowel Consonant (VC) and Consonant Vowel Consonant (CVC) words.

PRACTICAL TASK
What are the definitions of 'phoneme' and 'grapheme'? How many phonemes are there in spoken English?

Phase 3

This phase completes the letters of the alphabet. It also introduces sounds represented by more than one letter, for example 'oa', 'ow' and 'ar'. Children also continue to practise CVC blending and segmenting, and also apply this knowledge to reading and spelling two-syllable words and captions.

Phase 4

In this phase, children consolidate their knowledge of graphemes in reading and spelling words containing adjacent consonants; examples of these are 'jump', 'went' and 'frog'.

Phase 5

The purpose of this phase is to broaden the children's knowledge of graphemes and phonemes for use in reading and spelling. They learn new graphemes and alternative pronunciations for these. An example of this is 'ow' – cow, blow.

Phase 6

By the time children reach this phase, they should be able to read hundreds of words. During this phase, children become fluent readers and increasingly accurate spellers. It is also focused on looking more at word-specific spellings and making choices between spelling alternatives.

Having detailed briefly the different phases of Letters and Sounds, below is the sequence of teaching for each discrete phonics session of Phase 3.

Introduction
- Objectives and criteria for success.

Revisit and review
- Practise previously learned letters or graphemes.

Teach
- Teach new graphemes.
- Teach one or two tricky words.

Practise
- Practise blending and reading words with a new Grapheme–Phoneme Correspondence (GPC).
- Practise segmenting and spelling words with a new GPC.

Apply
- Read or write a caption or sentence using one or more tricky words and words containing the graphemes.

Assess learning against criteria

REFLECTIVE TASK

Observe a phonics session in your setting, noting the pace of the session and progression made by the children during it. Reflect on the phonics approaches taught within your school setting.

The next section of the chapter will discuss in detail aspect 3 of the *Rose Review* (2006): intervention programmes for children displaying reading difficulties.

Children experiencing reading difficulties

For many years, experts have studied to find reasons why children experience reading difficulties. For many teachers, children's failure to make good progress in reading is a main area of concern. Browne (2002, p191) comments on how the difficulties manifest themselves in a number of ways and points out that some children may have several types of difficulty. She explains this further by stating that, until the reading difficulty and its cause have been analysed, it is hard to provide the appropriate help and support. Browne found five possible types of reading difficulty (Browne, 2002, p192); these are:

1. being unable to read;
2. not wanting to read;
3. not understanding what is read;
4. thinking one can't read;
5. not reading the texts provided.

But questions may be asked as to what causes these types of reading difficulties. Browne identifies three sets of possible factors that often contribute to failure in learning to read (Browne, 2002, p192). The following demonstrates these factors.

Physical factors
- Visual impairment.
- Hearing problems.
- Language delay or disorder.
- Ill health resulting in prolonged or frequent absence from school.
- Environmental factors.
- High adult expectations and pressure.
- Absence of books at home.
- Unfavourable home circumstances.

School factors
- Irrelevant materials.
- Teacher expectations too high.
- Teacher expectations too low.
- Purpose for reading not clear to the children.
- Poorly organised reading programme.
- Teachers responding negatively to children who are slow to start reading.

Personal characteristics
- Anxiety.
- Lack of motivation.
- Short attention span.
- Poor self-image.
- Not understanding what reading is for.
- General learning difficulties.

REFLECTIVE TASK

Think of a child in your setting who you feel is experiencing reading difficulties. Using the list above, can you identify any possible factors that could contribute to this?

Myers and Burnett (2004) agree with Browne (2002) in that, when children display difficulties in reading, this limits their access to literature and the wider curriculum. Like Browne, they also identify some of the problems children have with reading; these include lack of:

- interest;
- confidence;
- phonic skills;
- reading for meaning;
- the ability to recall letters and high-frequency words.

It is essential that children escape this cycle of failure and experience the pleasures of reading and a sense of achievement. In any classroom there will be a wide variety of learning styles, barriers to learning and support needs, for which effective provision must be made (McKay, 2004). It is important for professionals to recognise and respond effectively to the learning needs of children, providing additional support when necessary. There are many ways in which reading difficulties can be overcome, but these involve careful planning of tasks, selection of texts and the provision of support. Children can then see that reading is a meaningful activity (Myers and Burnett, 2004, p221). Many of the contributing factors outlined above can be corrected; for example, physical factors can often be corrected or helped by referring the child for a sight or hearing test. Other physical problems need to be addressed individually, but this does not mean that the child cannot or will not read. Environmental difficulties may be solved by the school working closely with the parents and carers in order to find ways to help the child to read and develop interests in reading.

REFLECTIVE TASK

Think of a child who is making good progress in reading. Why do you think that is? Compare these factors with a child who is experiencing reading difficulties. What are the differences? What steps could you put in place to help overcome these?

Myers and Burnett (2004, p222) offered suggestions for supporting children with reading difficulties.

Supporting children who lack interest, enthusiasm and confidence in reading
This can be encouraged through:
- frequent reading aloud by the teacher of a wide range of texts;
- provision of carefully selected texts that relate to children's interests;
- opportunities to read to younger children;
- opportunities to share books with friends and listen to tapes.

Supporting children in reading for meaning
This can be encouraged through:
- opportunities to share and discuss texts of interest with friends;
- close procedure and activities to develop responses;
- focused activities of interest, such as a headline for a newspaper report, an e-mail or a text message to a friend.

Supporting children in recalling letters and recognising high-frequency words
Developing visual discrimination can be encouraged through:
- matching games, snap or bingo;
- discussing shapes of letters and words;
- highlighting a letter or high-frequency word in a text;
- locating examples of letters and high-frequency words in shared texts.

Hence, Goouch and Lambirth (2011: 31) offer some good practice suggestions for teaching reading for shared and guided reading:

- identify features of print;
- instruct children in relation to phonics;
- use multi-sensory approaches – visual aids;
- model ways of reading print;

- use the opportunity to maximise connections with children's prior experiences and existing knowledge;
- create activities in which children can collaborate to read and write.

> **PRACTICAL TASK**
>
> Consider the support strategies above to help readers and choose one from each section. Devise a short practical task for each that you could use to implement these.

In view of Myers and Burnett's (2004) findings on how the lack of phonic skills can cause children to have reading difficulties, the Rose Review (DfES, 2006) also acknowledged and analysed that high-quality phonics teaching was needed to help children make progress in their reading. This was highlighted in aspect 3 of their findings. Evidence for the importance of synthetic phonics in tackling literacy difficulties has also been advocated by Ehri et al. (2001) and in 2005, Johnston and Watson revealed the teaching of synthetic phonics as having a *major and long lasting effect on children's reading and spelling attainment* (2005, 9 p12).

The Rose Review (DfES, 2006) recommends that synthetic phonics teaching forms the basis of early literacy teaching. The resources used should accommodate a range of learning styles to meet the needs of all children in order for them to access the phonics programme. There should be intervention programmes in place to support children who are experiencing difficulties with reading. In the review (cited in Litterick, 2006), Rose refers to the 'three waves', which the *SEN Code of Practice* (DfES, 2001) describes as a 'graduated response' to identifying and meeting SEN, and relates them to teaching and intervention to support children with significant literacy difficulties.

The Waves of Intervention model

Wave 1 The effective inclusion of all children in daily, 'quality-first teaching.'
Wave 1 is about what should be on offer for all children: the effective inclusion of all pupils in high quality everyday personalised teaching. Such teaching will, for example, be bases on clear objectives that are shared with the children and returned to at the end of the lesson: carefully explain new vocabulary; use lively, interactive teaching styles and make maximum use of visual and kinaesthetic as well as auditory/verbal learning. Approaches like these are the best way to reduce, from the start, the number of children who need extra help with their learning of behaviour.

(DCFS, 2008)

Wave 2 Additional intervention to enable children to work at age-related expectations or above.
Defined as targeted small-group, short-term structured intervention for pupils who can be expected to catch up with their peers. (DCFS, 2008)

Wave 3 Additional, highly personalised interventions, for example specifically targeted approaches for children identified as requiring SEN support (on School Action, School Action Plus or with a statement of SEN). This intervention may need to be a more intensive programme, involving more individual support or specialist expertise. (DCFS, 2008)

Early intervention to support the foundations of reading is necessary. As advocated by Rose (2006) a tiered approach to intervention makes sense, whereby accommodations are first made to high-quality mainstream teaching and then more specific interventions are delivered (Snowling and Hulme, 2010).

Brooks (2002) researched the effectiveness of intervention schemes. He published the findings in his report *What Works for Children with Literacy Difficulties*. The intention of the report was to provide clear information on schemes available in order to inform practice and offer choices of approach (Brooks, 2002). The majority of the intervention schemes he researched were 'wave 3' programmes, although some were being used at the 'wave 2' stage. This involved analysing 25 different schemes, as he found many local authorities were using dissimilar programmes. Examples of these include: *Better Reading Partnership*, originally developed in Bradford; *Reading Recovery*, which is being used in many local authorities across the UK; the *Knowsley Reading Project*; and *Paired Reading* in Kirklees. He analysed how effective these schemes were in helping children to progress with their reading. The examples above found that children made progress with their reading after taking part in the intervention programmes.

REFLECTIVE TASK

Think about your setting. What intervention programmes are in place to help children with reading difficulties? How do you measure their progress?

CHAPTER SUMMARY

- There are many different theories and practice concerned with the development of reading.
- The Rose Review brought about changes to phonics teaching, early literacy teaching and early reading.
- There are many intervention programmes in place across the UK to help children with reading difficulties.

REFERENCES

Adams, M.J. (1990) *Beginning to Read: Thinking and learning about print*. Cambridge, MA: MIT Press.

Augur, J. and Briggs, S. (1992) Hickey *Multi-Sensory Language Course*. London: Whurr Publishers.

Brooks, G. (2002) What Works for Children with Literacy Difficulties? London: DfES.

Browne, A. (2002) *Developing Language and Literacy 3–8*. London: Paul Chapman.

Cremin, T. in Goouch, K and Lambirth, A. (2008) *Understanding Phonics and the Teaching of Reading: Critical perspectives*. Buckingham: Open University Press.

Department for Children, Schools and Families (DCSF) (2008) *Early Years Foundation Stage*. Available online at www.education.gov.uk/publications/standard/publicationDetail/ Page1/DCSF-00261–2008 (accessed 1/3/12).

Department for Children, Schools and Families (DCSF) (2008) *The National Strategies: Secondary*. Available online at http://dera.ioe.ac.uk/2516/1/sec_app_senr_leader_ guidance.pdf (accessed 1/3/12).

Department for Education (2008) *Early Years Foundation Stage*. Available online at www.education.gov.uk/publications/standard/publicationDetail/Page1/DCSF. Ref no. DCSF-00261-2008 (accessed 20/3/12).

Department for Education and Employment (1999) *Progression in Phonics*. London: DfEE.

Department for Education and Employment (DfEE) (2000) *Curriculum Guidance for the Foundation Stage*. London: QCA.

Department for Education and Skills (DfES) (2001) *SEN Code of Practice*. Nottingham: Crown.

Department for Education and Skills (DfES) (2006) *Independent Review of the Teaching of Early Reading: Final report*. Nottingham: DfES.

Department for Education and Skills (DfES) (2007) *Letters and Sounds: Principles and practice of high quality phonics*. London: DfES.

Dombey, H. (2009) *The Simple View of Reading. ITE English: Readings for discussion*. www.ite.org.uk/ite_readings/simple_view_reading.pdf (accessed 1/3/12).

Ehri, L., Nunes, S., Willows, D. Schuster, B., Yaghoub-Zadeh, Z. and Shanahan, T. (2001) Phonemic awareness instruction helps children learn to read: evidence from the National Reading Panel's meta-analysis, *Reading Research Quarterly*, 36: 250–87.

Ehri, L. C. (2005) Development of sight word reading: phases and findings in Snowling, M. J. and Hulme, C. (eds) *The Science of Reading: A handbook*. Oxford: Blackwell Publishing.

Goouch, K. and Lambirth, A. (2011) *Teaching Early Reading and Phonics: Creative approaches to early literacy*. London: SAGE Publications.

Goswamin, U. (2008) Reading, complexity and the brain. *Literacy*, 42 (2): 67–74.

Hall, K. (2003) *Listening to Stephen Read: Multiple perspectives on literacy*, Milton Keynes: Open University Press.

Hickey, R. (2009) *33 Ways to Help with Reading. Supporting children who struggle with basic skills*. Oxford: Routledge.

House of Commons Education and Skills Committee (2004) *Teaching Children to Read*. London: TSO.

Johnston, R. and Watson, J. (2005) *A Seven Year Study of the Effects of Synthetic Phonics Teaching on Reading and Spelling Attainment*. Available online at www.scotland.gov.uk/Publications/ 2005/02/20682/52383 (accessed 30/8/08).

Johnston, R. and Watson, J. (2007) *Teaching Synthetic Phonics*. Exeter: Learning Matters.

Lewis, M. and Ellis, S. (Eds) (2006) *Phonics: Practice, Research and Policy*. London: Paul Chapman.

Litterick, I. (2006) *How can Technology Help with Phonics?* Available online at www.dyslexic. com/phonics (accessed 14/9/08).

Lloyd, S. and Wernham, S. (2005) Jolly Phonics. Available online at www.jollylearning.co.uk/ (accessed 20/11/08).

Lockwood, M. (2008) *Promoting Reading for Pleasure in the Primary School*. London: SAGE Publications.

McKay, N. (2004) The case for dyslexia friendly schools, in Reid, G. and Fawcett, A. (eds) *Dyslexia in Context: Research, policy and practice*. London: Whurr.

Myers, J. and Burnett, C. (2004) *Teaching English 3–11*. London: Continuum.

Nutbrown, C (2006) *Key Concepts in Early Childhood Education and Care*. Thousand Oaks, CA: SAGE Publications.

Port, R. (2006) The graphical basis of phones and phonemes, in Munro, M. And Schwen-Bohn, O. (eds) *Second Language Speech Learning: The role of language experience in speech perception and production*. Amsterdam: John Benjamins.

Reid, G. (2003) *Dyslexia: A Practitioner's Handbook*. 3rd edition. Chichester: Wiley.

Rose, J. (2006) *Independent Review of the Teaching of Early Reading*. Report reference DfES-0201-2006. London: DfES.

Smith, F. (1976) Learning to read by reading. *Language Arts*, 53: 297–9, 322.

Snowling, M.J. and Hulme, C. (2010) Evidence-based interventions for reading and language difficulties: creating a virtuous circle, *British Journal of Educational Psychology*.

Snowling, M.J. and Hulme, C. (eds) (2007) *The Science of Reading: A handbook*. Oxford: Blackwell.

Vellutino, F., Fletcher, J., Snowling, M. and Scanlon, M. (2004) Specific reading disability (dyslexia): what have we learned in the past four decades?, *Journal of Child Psychology*, 45 (1): 2–40.

FURTHER READING

Lewis, M. and Ellis, S. (eds) (2006) *Phonics: Practice, research and policy*. London: Paul Chapman.

Ruttle, K. (2009) *You Can Motivate Reluctant Readers*. Warwickshire: Scholastic.

10 SUPPORTING PUPILS THROUGH CRISIS

Gillian Goddard

CHAPTER OBJECTIVES

By the end of this chapter you will:

- have greater awareness of the impact of life crises on pupils' education and well-being;

- understand the importance of resilience and how to develop that in pupils;

- be able to offer support to pupils through challenging times;

- be able to assess your own limitations in support and to decide when a pupil needs referral to outside or internal professional support or health services.

LINKS TO **HLTA** STANDARDS

1. Understand the key factors that affect children's and young people's learning and progress.

2. Know how to contribute to effective personalised provision by taking practical account of diversity.

3. Establish fair, respectful, trusting, supportive and constructive relationships with children and young people.

4. Communicate effectively and sensitively with children, young people, colleagues, parents and carers.

5. Recognise and respect the contribution that parents and carers can make to the development and well-being of children and young people.

6. Demonstrate the commitment to collaborative and cooperative working with colleagues.

7. Know how other frameworks that support the development and well-being of children and young people impact on their practice.

Introduction

The emotional wellbeing and mental health of our children and young people is vital – to them as individuals and to all of us. Failing to tackle emotional problems and mental disorders as early as possible creates significant social and economic costs. The presence of mental illness during childhood has been show to lead to costs which are up to ten times higher during adulthood.

(National Advisory Council for Children's Mental Health and Psychological Wellbeing, 2010, p3)

In a similar vein, Newman (2002) argues that, although physical health in children in the Western world has got better and better over the previous century, mental health problems among the young have not:

on the contrary, a substantial increase in psycho-social disorders of children has taken place in most developed countries of the past half century, including suicide and para-suicide, self-injurious behaviour, conduct eating disorders and depression.

(Newman, 2002, cited in Johnson, 2008, p385)

It is of no surprise that schools are mandated through the Every Child Matters outcomes (DFES, 2003) and through subsequent Government policy to play an active part in promoting the psychological well-being of their pupils and for supporting pupils through life crises (DCSF, 2010; NICE, 2008; DfES, 2001). Much of this work falls to the support staff in the school, though teachers and the head ultimately have responsibility for the health and well-being of the pupils. Support staff, in their professional capacity to provide pastoral support, are frequently expected to spot problems early, enquire, report to teaching staff, liaise with parents and carers, refer on if necessary, but also sometimes, to plan and deliver one-to-one or small-group interventions to support and assist pupils through their difficulties (NICE, 2008). Learning mentors usually have a primary responsibility in this field but many TAs in class help children going through tough times simply by their caring attitude, their timely kind advice and their ability to listen. This is also true of lunchtime welfare staff.

It may seem strange to consider that coping with a life crisis can affect one's mental health but in reality, problems resulting from life crises can lead pupils to be depressed, demotivated, irrationally angry and unhappy, potentially to the point of suicide. All of these powerful emotional states will impact detrimentally on the pupil's psychological well-being and also their educational attainment (NICE, 2008). For these reasons alone, this chapter will be dedicated to understanding the issue of life crises and the role of support staff in helping pupils through these troubled times.

The impact of life crisis

All of us at some time or another have experienced major crises in our lives. Pupils are no different. Your own work with children and young people will verify that some children have lives battered by either continuous or sporadic episodes of grave misfortune, the type that would break a strong adult.

REFLECTIVE TASK

Take a few minutes to consider your own life and those times of great crisis or trauma. Identify what types of event caused those.

Now consider children's life crises as you have experienced these. List the types of life situations that can cause a crisis for pupils.

Life crises and their impact on the pupil

Crises in life often revolve around loss, trauma, violence, illness, insecurity and/or fear. Pupils can experience greater impact from crisis:

- because they are young and have little experience of life to relate to the crisis (this is especially true of those of primary or younger age who are still developing cognitively and simply do not understand what is happening around them);
- because those in adolescence are simultaneously undergoing the hormonally driven emotional chaos of puberty;
- because of their relative powerlessness to change events or take control of them, or their own lives;
- because of their dependence for survival and care of others who may also be affected by this life crisis.

Powerful, fearful and painful emotions can dominate during times of crisis. The sense of powerlessness can cause despair and deep anger and frustration. It is the force of these emotions and the length of time that they may have to be endured that produces a high risk of longer term harm. Children who are already vulnerable by virtue of learning difficulty, developmental delay, communication difficulties, prior trauma and loss through bereavement and divorce or becoming 'looked after', experience of abuse or severe bullying, those with chronic physical or mental health difficulties and those with no friends, low self-esteem and/or a history of academic failure are more likely to suffer badly during a further life crisis, though this is not always so (see later) (DfES, 2001; Stokes, 2009).

REFLECTIVE TASK

Go back to your reflection on your own experience of life crises. Think back to the last time you were facing a life crisis or really troubled time.

- What were your feelings at this time?
- What helped you? What made things worse?

Emotions that come up from work with children and young people experiencing difficulties with grief, loss and trauma tend to be anger, confusion, fear, insecurity, powerlessness, a sense of helplessness, low self-esteem, depression, unhappiness, rejection of life and relationships, and a fear of trusting anyone (especially when loss has been an issue, such as through bereavement or parental separation) (Jigsaw4u, 2011; Winston's Wish, 2011).

Things that help are:

- developing, or being taught, strategies to manage these emotions;
- accepting friends who listen and distract you from your problems;
- family/community support;
- someone to listen and the chance to 'talk out' or express feelings and have those acknowledged;
- practical small ways to gain some control in life;
- practical help to make things easier in daily life;
- help to see things positively;
- lots of praise.

Support staff can provide many of these and substitute for some of these when, for example, family support is absent.

Look at these studies and try to identify what each child is likely to be feeling and how the school could help.

CASE STUDY 1: MICHAEL (AGE 14)

Michael comes from a family with three other siblings and a lone parent. He has just been diagnosed as having macular degeneration. It was quite sudden in its onset but he is steadily going blind. It is untreatable. The consultant spoke to him with his parents yesterday and explained what was wrong and what would happen to him. He was quiet throughout and asked no questions. His mother was distressed and he felt he was to blame for her upset. The doctor said he will be receiving some help from the hospital to learn Braille at a time when it can be arranged and was the right time. Michael has loads of friends and he is a talented footballer and member of the school team.

- *What is Michael likely to be feeling / experiencing?*
- *How is he likely to behave in school?*
- *How is his academic performance going to be affected at this point?*
- *What are his immediate emotional needs, now in the longer term?*
- *How could the school meet his needs and help him through this life crisis?*

CASE STUDY 2: ZENAT (AGED 7)

Zenat has just arrived in this country with her parents and younger brother. They are refugees and asylum seekers from a war-torn country. They were in a detention centre first for several weeks, then their asylum application was accepted (her parents had both undergone periods of arrest and torture for political and religious opposition to the regime). They were transferred to a north-west city and put in flat in a tower block on an estate. Zenat was brought to school today for the first time by a refugee support worker. She has already learned a little English at the detention centre. Her parents are frightened and lost, and stay with her baby brother in the flat all the time.

- *What is Zenat likely to be feeling / experiencing?*
- *How is she likely to behave in school?*
- *How well will she cope with school work?*
- *What are her emotional needs immediately and in the longer term?*
- *How could the school meet her needs and help her get through this life crisis?*

Both Zenat and Michael need a key person to build up a confidential and supportive relationship with, someone who can help them not only practically but also emotionally, someone they can depend on. They both need help with communicating their feelings and letting go of them. They need safety and routine, which may mean making sure they are given advance warning of changes to school routines. The support of friends who accept them as they are and as they might become is vital. Zenat doesn't have that yet. Michael may have friends though his friendships may be dependent for their durability on his success on the football field. It may be that both will need an 'organised' circle of friends brought in to support them, peers who are by their nature supportive, accepting and generous of heart and spirit.

Short-term personal goals for these two students need to be set, in which they may persevere and triumph. Both may well benefit from meeting up with other children or adults in their situation but who are further along in their adjustment (for example, in Michael's case with a member of the Olympic blind football squad). They may need simple practical aids and facilities, bilingual resources or enlarged print, access to technology and specialist input from experts who can help them bridge the gap from their pervious world to this new one (Visual Impairment Support and English as an Alternative Language (EAL)). They both probably would benefit from parental liaison, even if it means going to the parent's flat to talk. Did you have any of these in your responses?

Often pupils only need the offer of help and knowledge that support strategies have been put into place to get through bad times. It is remarkable how resilient and adaptable children are. However, this adaptability and resilience can never be assumed for where it is assumed and nothing is done, pupils can suffer grievously, often in isolation.

Developing and supporting resilience

Resilience can be defined as the ability to recover from crisis even though this crisis is so bad that it would usually result in major emotional or psychological hurt, for example, suffering a serious injury that impairs your functions, bereavement of someone really important to you, being abused over a period of time, or being rendered homeless with nowhere to go, or having to flee your country and seek asylum in a completely different one with a radically different culture, climate and language (Stokes, 2009; Clinton, 2008; Johnson, 2008; Ungar, 2008).

Resilience isn't just an ability to bounce back to a normal way of living but a capacity to learn from the trauma and become stronger psychologically (Clinton, 2008). This comes through knowledge and celebration of one's own survival: 'If I came though that I can come through anything', by the development of a series of skills that help the person cope during times of trial and confidence in one's own strength. This is reinforced in Stokes' (2009) chapter on resilience in bereaved children where she discusses the states of mind of children and young people who have survived bereavement. The children are stronger in some of her case studies and broken in others, but all are altered by the challenges and terrible pain of bereavement.

Many people believe that resilience is an innate quality, to paraphrase that song lyric (to avoid copyright infringement) when the life gets rough, the tough swing into action, but this isn't born out in research evidence (Masten, 2001; Rutter, 1990; Clinton, 2008). Instead, it seems to be a mix of innate personal qualities and outside elements of support that surround the person (Johnson, 2008). This is where schools and support staff can help.

Summarising from the combined research of Clinton (2008), Ungar (2008), Stokes (2009) and Grotberg (2001), the following personal or internal qualities and skills are seen in children who demonstrate resilience to life's disasters:

- self-worth levels are normally high;
- an easy-going personality;
- an optimistic outlook;
- self-belief in one's own ability to cope;
- self-motivated;
- large repertoire of interpersonal skills;
- popular/attractive with others (this makes you more likely to get support from others);
- intelligence /cognitive aptitude;
- ability to reflect on life experience and learn from that.

Internal factors are only part of the story, however. Outside factors matter too. First and foremost, in times of crisis people tend to draw on family support. Did you have that on your list of things that helped you through times of crisis? Clinton (2008) and Rutter (1987) have both identified the helpful elements of family support when needing to develop resilience. These are open and honest communication between family members, a sense of family unity as a strength (we will all stick together), a family that is capable of adjusting to new ways and different circumstances, usually by holding on to core strengths like family identity and love, and letting go of other things that matter less (quality of housing, possessions, job status, success) (Clinton, 2008). In addition, Rutter (1987) suggests that to be resilient a person needs a special relationship with someone they love, rather than just a general acceptance of a place in the family. We need someone to care for us in a deep and enduring way.

Finally, the environment we live in and experience daily can also make a difference to our ability to cope. Community, religious or cultural identity, if strong, can provide that sense of mutual support and strength (Johnson, 2008). We feel we belong and therefore are not alone when facing these difficulties. Schools form part of this collective identity. They also give the pupil a place to escape from their problems for a few hours and a chance to succeed, despite their troubles (Rutter, 1987; Johnson, 2008). This is also true of taking part in personal hobbies and interests that take the child away from their problems and help them to enjoy themselves (Stokes, 2009). Good solid friendships come high on the list of outside factors that are influential in coming through a crisis (Ungar, 2008). Again, go back to your list and see if this featured on your 'helpful' list. Finally, Ungar (2008) mentions the place and benefit of official professional interventions from Government agencies or voluntary organisations such as victim support groups or *Team Around the Child* (TAC) (DfE, 2011a).

REFLECTIVE TASK

Consider now your experience of your own times of trial and your experiences of other children and adults who have really struggled when bad troubles come. Write down the types of characteristics that might be present in their lives that would make it far more difficult for them to show resilience. Remember to consider outside factors as well as internal dispositions.

In a research study conducted by Johnson (2008), tracking the experiences and reactions of vulnerable 9–12-year-olds in Australia (those who had already been traumatised or experienced life difficulties) over a period of eight years he found that there were certain risk factors that teachers could identify early in children and thus plan interventions for, by providing for extra levels of personal support and curriculum work on resilience development. He discovered that children who struggled more when facing crisis appeared to be:

- *socially isolated with few friends;*
- *negative about themselves;*
- *unable to accept responsibility for making choices in life;*
- *victim orientated (blame others for their predicament);*
- *impulsive, unpredictable, and sometimes violent;*
- *disengaged from school life;*
- *present orientated (i.e. live for today with little regard for the future);*
- *easily led;*
- *unrealistic about goals and plans.*

(adapted from Johnson, 2008, p398)

REFLECTIVE TASK
Does this match your experience of similar children?

It is important for support staff and teachers not to 'blame' the child for being this way and therefore opt out of offering any kind of sympathy or support. It might well be that the sum total of a child's reactions to crisis are unhelpful in the long run, but children and adults who behave this way are trying to keep safe, to survive, usually by either lying low or kicking out. Their attitudes and behaviours are the product of their life experiences and learned from these. Consequently, they see the world as a dangerous, unfair, lonely and brutal place. They often feel powerless to change this or themselves; indeed, they cannot see why they should since everything will always go to the bad in their lives. It takes time, patience and relentless positivity on the part of support staff working with these children to help them see things differently, believe in themselves and others, and take control of their lives in no matter how small a way.

Reactive approaches to helping a child in crisis / Rutter's (1990) protective processes

Reduction of risk impact

Support strategies for a child experiencing resilience difficulties are very similar (for obvious reasons) to those discussed earlier, but Rutter (1990) points out that there are some essential things that can be put in place to help a child with low levels of resilience. He referred to these as protective processes. The first seems self-evident but it is often forgotten. We are so busy helping a child come through a tough crisis that we forget that we may be able to stop the crisis all together, or at least reduce its severity. If a child is in a risky and dangerous situation, then getting a child away from that could be the answer, even if it means putting into place a course of action that leads to them entering state care. An example of this can be seen in this case study, which is taken from real life though anonymised.

Case Study 3: Paul

Paul is nine. His only carer is his mother, who is addicted to illegal drugs and who has to work as a prostitute to get the money she needs to support her habit. Paul has two younger siblings, under school age, half brother and sister. He looks after them when mum is out. Sometimes he comes home from school and the door is locked and he can't get in. His younger siblings are outside playing or waiting unattended. When this happens he knows his mother has brought a man to the flat and doesn't want the children to disturb her.

Paul is always hungry and has been known to steal food from other children. He doesn't bring his dinner money at all regularly. The school has taken to furnishing him with food whether he pays or not. He is smelly and wears very old, ill-fitting clothes. The school welfare officer fails to gain access to the flat when mum is there, though mostly she is out when he calls. Paul never misses school, no matter how poorly he is. It is warm, safe and he gets food. He can be violent and is very low achieving. He sometimes falls asleep in class. A class teacher, coming home from the theatre one night sees Paul in the subway in town begging and offering himself for prostitution to men passing by. He tells Paul to go home or he will call the police.

Finally, social services are called by the school, but they perceive Paul as too low a risk to intervene urgently as he is attending school and being fed, and as there have been no actual incidents of his prostitution. The family will be visited when a social worker becomes free.

The school then takes a risk and contacts the grandmother of Paul (who lives a long way away but is given as a second next of kin). She is the mother of Paul's father (he had left Paul's mum ages ago when she was pregnant, but he knew of Paul's birth). His former girlfriend had refused all contact and he had long given up on trying to see his son. The school explain to the grandmother over the phone their concerns and ask if Paul's father could contact them and help. Remarkably, Paul's father (who was married and had a child of his own) immediately visits his former girlfriend and, with her full agreement, takes Paul back to his own family, where he now lives. Social Services visited the family a few weeks later and removed the younger siblings into care when mum refused to cooperate with any family care support or addiction help. Mum was relieved the children had gone.

This is an example of intervention to take the child out of harm's way, out of the crisis. Separation carries with it its own troubles but Paul is now cared for, his needs are being met and he is growing to love and be loved by his family. He misses his siblings, but that too is a relief for him, as he is no longer responsible for them.

At a simpler level, stopping a crisis may put a stop to persistent bullying in school to remove a child from harm, rather than teaching him to cope by living with persistent bullying.

Rutter (1990) also identified the need in this type of approach to help the child to be less frightened of the situation they are in. A pupil may be disproportionately worried and anxious about a situation because of past bad experience. This happens frequently with the death of an adult carer. If a pupil's mother dies, it seems a real and present danger that their father will die suddenly too. Children can become really scared to the point of paralysis because they fear this. A simple strategy like letting the pupil phone an agreed number to speak for a couple of minutes to their father can help the child to be less anxious and build up new experiences of the continued dependable presence of their father. Being able to speak about their fears and to be reasoned with is also valuable. For this, a child needs a trusted member of staff who can take time to listen to them and who is kind and positive in their response.

Reduction of negative chain reactions

This reactive approach centres on getting help for the child and/or the family in the crisis situation to stop things getting worse. It might, for example, be the bringing in of CAMHS (Child and Adolescent Mental Health Services) or a charity to support the family through the problems, such as Jigsaw4u, which supports children and young people through grief, loss and trauma. It can also mean simply giving a child an outlet for their troubles by listening to them and offering them a safe haven, such as a quiet room or a place in the quiet area, when things get bad.

Self-esteem/ self-efficacy work

This involves planned interventions to raise the pupil's self-esteem and, even more significantly in times of crisis, to raise their confidence in their own ability to get through this. Self-belief centres on an understanding of what children have in their own 'resource box' to get through this time. Work can focus on getting the pupils to consciously identify their own valuable qualities inside themselves that will help (Grotberg's (2001) protective factors). These are 'I am' factors, for example 'I am strong', 'I am lovable'. Pupils also identify the resources they have around them to draw on, the 'I have' factors ('I have people around me who will help', 'I have friends who will support me'). Finally, they identify their own skills, the 'I can' factors. These could be, for example, 'I can ask for help', 'I can solve problems' or 'I can control myself when I get angry or upset'.

Counting what you have in your armoury to cope rather than what you do not have is crucial to the development of a resilient attitude.

Opportunities to regain control in their own lives

Rutter (1990) adds this to his list of reactive strategies. Schools can actively encourage the pupil in difficulties to make their own decisions about small things. This could be simply offering support and letting the pupil determine when and how that is offered. For example, 'if you feel you want to come in from break/lunch and do some quiet reading in here, then that is fine. Just come in when you feel you need that'. Here the pupil is in control of accessing the best place to suit his/her mood needs. This is often practised as an anger management strategy and achieves the same thing, self-control, self-determination. Being aware that you can manage your life and your moods by actively doing something (a calming action; removal from the aggravating situation; asking for help; journaling; being assertive) empowers you and helps you to feel that your feet are back on solid ground. There are multiple situations when small choices can be offered to pupils that do not disadvantage others, but do empower the child. It is remarkable how little is needed in terms of decision-making to feel better, stronger and more in control.

Teaching resilience strategies and attitudes before there is a crisis (pro-active)

When a pupil is in crisis, reactive approaches are needed to respond to the child's individual needs. However, it is also valuable to build in resilience development within the personal, social and health education (PSHE) curriculum as a way of preparing pupils to cope with future life crises. This section will discuss pro-active ways of helping pupils cope with and come back from adversity.

Classroom ethos

The cultivated prevailing ethos in a classroom or school really does affect the resilience levels of pupils (and staff). In a classroom an attitude of adventure in learning, trying hard and risk-taking when mistakes are viewed as opportunities to learn, really helps. Alternatively, if academic failure is deemed unacceptable and success is hunted down with crushing forensic efficiency, then when a child comes up against a problem in their own lives or that of school learning, they will fear failure and that failure will be a catastrophe, because that is what the teacher has taught them. By developing an atmosphere where the pupils help one another and know it is okay to openly admit you need help will benefit children. It will help them to trust in others and seek help when things are difficult rather than fear it and hide from such admissions.

Self-help strategies

Strategies can be taught that are self-help ones, both for learning and in mood-management. 'What do I do if. . .?' can be explored and rehearsed in circle time or role play. These can be enhanced with problem-solving games and activities which encourage independent thinking and also collective decision-making and group interdependence.

Self-esteem based on sound self-awareness

Pupils are far more resilient if they have good levels of self-esteem, based on realistic self-awareness. All children can feel good about themselves because they all possess some talents, skills, aptitudes and qualities that can be praised, acknowledged and celebrated together. These may not be obviously academic but 'trying hard' and 'never giving up' are invaluable to life and learning, so these can be praised and valued. Being kind is also invaluable in life. Staff need to find things that are good in each pupil to help them recognise their own worth. Other pupils also need to be able to recognise the worth in all and celebrate that. Rather than allowing pupils to put one another down, staff should encourage pupils to raise one another up, by focusing on each other's strengths.

Autonomy

Developing independence is also a successful strategy to assist in resilience formation. Promoting personal responsibility and ownership of behaviours and actions actually empowers the child. A pupil is less dependent on the judgement and arbitration of adults to resolve difficulties. They are not passive but active in finding resolutions and in representing their own views in assertive engagements. Non-violent conflict resolution processes enhance this, enabling pupils to come to some agreed solution to conflict between each other (with the aid of peer facilitators) (Peer Mediation Network, 2011). This makes each party feel capable and responsible (Peer Mediation Network, 2011).

Humour

Humour is a major asset in being resilient. If you can laugh at your circumstances, it often feels less catastrophic. Humour in children needs to be helped to be funny rather than cruel. Its purpose is not to undermine others but to relax and let go of the gravity of the situation. Shared laughter is a powerful unifier and is frequently used as a social lubricant (Baron et al., 2007). Modelling humour is one of the key ways of teaching this.

A positive attitude

Perhaps the key factor in the cultivation of resilience is the adoption of a positive outlook, or optimistic attitude to life, even in the midst of difficulties. This 'glass half full' disposition is a challenge to adopt where, in general, feelings run to pessimism and are fuelled by fears which emphasise the worst possible anticipated outcomes. However, the recognition of what we have rather than what we don't have makes all the difference to cheering us up and predicating a positive outcome. This positive outlook can be modelled and practised in class with open expression of the good things that happened, the good things we feel and the good things we have to look forward to. Helping pupils to find something good in their situation will help them, as long as there is also an acknowledgement of the realities of the challenge facing them. Instead of just saying 'all will be well', one needs to say 'it's going to be tough but all will be well because you are adaptable, strong and we will help you.'

Modelling through stories and real life heroes

A rich diet in the classroom of stories involving people and children overcoming adversity can help to model resilience, especially if there is some focus on the strategies they used to help themselves rather than their natural qualities. Similarly, access to the accounts of real heroes face to face in class, where questions can be asked and humanity stressed, can also encourage pupils to grow and learn.

Resilience can be taught and caught but it is important to remember that individual life experiences from an early age can seriously undermine resilience in any person. The strongest person can be broken if successive crises follow on one from the other without recovery time, or if the loss is terrible and permanent. Ultimately, whether children are resilient or not, they need to be supported through times of trouble, by the provision of a special person who cares and can help, by a humane and empathic understanding of their situation and by practical arrangements that make life easier, albeit temporary ones, until things get better.

There are times, however, when the resources of the school or early years setting are insufficient to provide the help needed to children in crisis. Part of the skill in these situations is knowing when that point has been reached, especially if you are the key person supporting that individual. Knowledge of your limitations and those of the school are vital if harm is to be avoided. Similarly, a knowledge of what help is out there and how to access it is important. The recent development of genuinely integrated services and multi-professional support teams often help greatly in this situation (DfE, 2011b).

When to refer a pupil on

If a pupil undergoing a crisis, is showing signs of psychological disturbance that is getting worse, or is talking of suicide or even hinting at it, or is showing progressive signs of depression or disorganised, bizarre behaviour, then referral should be to either the GP of the pupil or to CAMHS (DCSF, 2010). This is done through the pastoral year leader or head teacher, or the SENCO. In most secondary schools, school counsellors are available and can help the key person with their concerns, or simply take the referral themselves and work with the pupil. In primary school, access to counselling is sometimes available but frequently not. The use of support from child support charities may be helpful for both phases of education, but parental involvement and permission are crucial. This can be problematic, but teachers and senior staff are the persons to handle this.

The most important thing to do professionally is to talk to someone who is responsible for the child in the school, normally the teacher or pastoral year leader, if you are anxious or worried at all. It is important that your concerns are communicated and responsibility shared. It also matters that in any referral, the pupil is told what is happening and any alteration of the type of support is explained. Pupils cope far better when they are involved in their health issues rather than rendered passive recipients of professional aid (Brom et al., 2008; NICE, 2008; DfES, 2001).

In conclusion

Pupils do experience really tough times in their young lives, but it is remarkable how resilient they are. Sometimes they only require the smallest of interventions to help them come successfully through their troubles. It behoves all adults working with children to offer that help morally, professionally and humanely and, if necessary, to bring in other professionals to assist when needed.

CHAPTER SUMMARY

- Emotional crises happen to children and young people, and often those they would turn to first, their families, may be also experiencing real difficulties and struggle to be able to help. It is therefore the school that can furnish the help that is needed.
- To do this the school needs to provide a key person who can be advocate, supporter and practical helper. This person needs to be able to listen and care for that pupil and offer practical advice.
- Resilience is needed to come through crises and end up with a positive outcome. Resilience is not just dependent on a person's character or qualities, but also on their environment and the support mechanisms they can draw on. These include family, community and friends. Having the chance to succeed in small things and have outside interests that can 'take the child away' from the problems for a short while, can help. Cultivating a positive attitude to life and being able to laugh at the situation also helps.
- Schools can teach and model resilient qualities and practise resilience strategies to equip pupils with the attitudes and skills needed to come through difficult times.

- It is important to know when a pupil's situation is becoming so bad that they need other professional help. Report all concerns to the designated person.
- Pupils always need to be involved in their own management and support, even if it is only in the form of an explanation rather than a choice.

REFERENCES

Baron, R. Byrne, D. and Branscombe, N. (2007) *Mastering Social Psychology*, London: Pearson.

Brom, D., Pat-Horenczyk, R. and Ford, J. (eds) (2008) *Treating Traumatised Children: Risk resilience and recovery.* New York: Routledge.

Clinton, J. (2008) Resilience and recovery, *International Journal of Children's Spirituality*, 13(3): 213–22.

Department for Children, Schools and Families (DCSF) (2010) *Keeping Children and Young People in Mind: The Government's full response to the independent review of CAMHS*, DCSF-01123–2009, London: DCSF.

Department for Education and Skills (DfES) (2001) *Promoting Children's Mental Health within Early Years and School Settings*. London: DfES.

Department for Education and Skills (DfES) (2003) *Every Child Matters Agenda*, London: DfES.

Department for Education (2011a) *Team Around the Child (TAC)*. Available at www.education.gov.uk/publications/standard/publicationdetail/page1/IW93/0709 (accessed 1/3/12).

Department for Education (2011b) *Integrated Working*. Available at www.education.gov.uk/childrenandyoungpeople/strategy/integratedworking/a0068938/integrated-working (accessed on 1/3/12).

Grotberg, E. (2001) Resilience programs for children in disaster, *Journal of Ambulatory Child Health*, 7: 75–83.

Jigsaw4u (2011) Available at www.jigsaw4u.org.uk (accessed 17/10/11).

Johnson, B. (2008) Teacher–Student relationships which promote resilience at school: a micro-level analysis of students views, *British Journal of Guidance & Counselling*, 36(4): 385–98.

Masten A. (2001) Ordinary magic: resilience processes in development, *American Psychologist*, 56: 227–38.

National Advisory Council for Children's Mental Health and Psychological Wellbeing (2010) *One Year On*, Report no. DCSF-00333–2010. Nottingham: DCSF.

National Institute for Health and Clinical Excellence (NICE) (2008) *Promoting Children's Social and Emotional Wellbeing in Primary Education*. London: NICE.

Newman, T. (2002*) Promoting Resilience: A review of effective strategies for child care services*, prepared for the Centre for Evidence-Based Social Services. Exeter: University of Exeter.

Peer Mediation Network (2011) Available at www.peermediationnetwork.org.uk/ (accessed 25/10/11).

Rutter, M. (1987) Psychological resilience and protective mechanisms, *American Journal of Orthopsychiatry*, 22: 323–56.

Rutter, M. (1990) Psychosocial resilience and protective mechanisms, in Rolf, J., Masten, A., Cicchetti, D., Nuechterlein, K. and Weintraub, S. (eds) *Risk and Protective Factors in the Development of Psychopathology*. New York: Cambridge University Press.

Stokes, J. (2009) Resilience and bereaved children, *Journal of Bereavement Care*, 28(1): 9–17.

Ungar, M. (2008) Resilience across cultures, *British Journal of Social Work*, 38: 218–35.

Winston's Wish Website (2011) Available online at www.winstonswish.org.uk (accessed 17/10/11).

11 SUPPORTING LEARNING IN THE EARLY YEARS

Jacqui Basquill

CHAPTER OBJECTIVES

By the end of this chapter you will:

- understand the current practice and theories linked to the Foundation Years;
- understand the many transitions a young child can go through, both within the school and outside and the effects this may have on their learning;
- be aware of the welfare requirements of the Foundation Stage.

LINKS TO **HLTA** STANDARDS

1. Have high expectations of children and young people with a commitment to helping them fulfil their potential.
2. Establish fair, respectful, trusting, supportive and constructive relationships with children and young people.
3. Demonstrate the positive values, attitudes and behaviour they expect from children and young people.
4. Communicate effectively and sensitively with children, young people, colleagues, parents and carers.
5. Recognise and respect the contribution that parents and carers can make to the development and well-being of children and young people.
6. Understand the key factors that affect children and young people's learning and progress.
7. Have sufficient understanding of their area(s) of expertise to support the development, learning and progress of children and young people.
8. Know how statutory and non-statutory frameworks for the school curriculum relate to the age and ability ranges of the learners they support.

Introduction

The earliest years in a child's life are absolutely critical. There is overwhelming international evidence that foundations are laid in the first years of life which, if weak, can have a permanent and detrimental impact on children's longer term development. A child's future choices, attainment, wellbeing, happiness and resilience are profoundly affected by the quality of the guidance, love and care they receive during these first years.

(Tickell, 2011, p2)

This chapter examines outstanding practice in the Foundation Years; it will help you to understand the underpinning theories and legislation that ensure all babies and young children receive the best possible start to learning. You will develop an understanding of the powerful effects transitions can have on a young child and consider how we can minimise the negative effects of these and ensure the child feels happy and confident with these transitions.

Finally, you will consider the welfare requirements in the Early Years Foundation Stage (EYFS) and how these can be assured.

Why are the Foundation Years different?

The importance of the Foundation Years has been highlighted in several recent reports. Field (2010) highlights the effects of child poverty and suggests that if these are not addressed within the first five years of life, there is little chance of improving the outcomes for the child. He emphasises that intervention needs to begin during pregnancy, educating and supporting the parents so that each child gets the best possible start in life. Fields discusses the key drivers of life chances; he identifies the significant factors at each stage of a child's development that have profound effects on the child's progress. This begins before birth and continues until adulthood. Allen (2011) gives in-depth explanations of why the Foundation Years are so significant, emphasising research findings that show that a child's developmental score at 22 months can serve as an accurate predictor of their educational outcomes at 26 years of age and that 'babies are born with 25 per cent of their brains developed, and there is then a rapid period of development so that by the age of three their brains are 80 per cent developed' (Allen, 2011, pxiii). It is clear from the findings of both of these reports that early intervention as soon as pregnancy is confirmed is essential if we are to ensure that all children are to have the support and opportunities to develop to their full potential, and become well-educated adults who can contribute fully to society.

Building on the findings of these reports Tickell (2011) in her review of the EYFS recommends that the new framework emphasises the role of the parents and carers as partners in their children's learning as well as an early report at age two to three years. She also suggests that this is linked to the health visitor's health and developmental review at aged two, thereby supporting professional relationships and sharing professional expertise regarding the progress the child is making.

REFLECTIVE TASK

Read the executive summaries of Frank Fields – *The Foundation Years: Preventing poor children from becoming poor adults* (Fields, 2010); Graham Allen – *Early Intervention: Next Steps* (Allen, 2011) and Claire Tickell – *The Early Years: Foundations for life, health and learning* (Tickell, 2011).

REFLECTIVE TASK

Consider the implications within your school; write a list of changes you think should be made to support the findings of these reports. What advantages and difficulties can you foresee with these? Discuss this with your mentor.

The Early Years Foundation Stage

The EYFS became statutory in 2008; it is a comprehensive framework supporting each child's development from birth to 60 months. While it has its faults, there is little doubt that the philosophy and principles it expounds have had a positive lasting effect on Early Years practice around the country.

The EYFS has two parts, Practice Guidance for the Early Years Foundation Stage and the Statutory Framework for the Early Years Foundation Stage. The first part gives practitioners support to deliver sound learning and developmental experiences for the children in their care.

The underpinning theory and principles are from research and good practice advocated by a variety of Early Years specialists, from both historical and modern times. There are four underpinning themes for the EYFS, each of which has an underpinning principle.

- *A unique child: every child is a competent learner from birth who can be resilient, capable, confident and self-assured.*
- *Positive relationships: children learn to be strong and independent from a base of loving and secure relationships with parents and/or a key person.*
- *Enabling environments: the environment plays a key role in supporting and extending children's development and learning.*
- *Learning and development: children develop and learn in different ways and at different rates and all areas of learning and development are equally important and interconnected.*

(DCSF, 2008, 1.10)

Each of these is further underpinned by four commitments which explain the aspects of each principle that the EYFS actively promotes practitioners to engage with. A recurring commitment for all four principles is that of reflective practice and this is a process in which all practitioners must engage.

Some of the earliest theories on childhood to be written were from the late seventeenth and early eighteenth centuries. Locke (1632–1704) described children as a 'tabula rasa' – a blank slate waiting to be filled with the knowledge imparted upon them by adults. He did acknowledge that children have natural predispositions and temperaments which would predispose them to certain skills and interests. His concept of early education was that the teacher would input knowledge and develop their natural skills and abilities (Gianoutsos, 2006). Rousseau (1712–1778), was a French philosopher who believed that children were naive and virtuous but were corrupted by the world. He believed that children should be protected and nurtured until the age of seven, and that they should be allowed to develop freely without constraints (Gianoutsos, 2006).

Other important theorists have contributed greatly to our understanding of early years learning. These include the following.

Friedrich Froebel (1782–1852) was a German educator who believed in supporting children to develop in harmony with nature. He used the term kindergarten – children's garden – instead of school as, in his opinion, young children needed to learn holistically in a natural environment, where adults would nurture them and encourage them to blossom. The gardens contained plots where children could grow plants and they were encouraged to work in pairs. Froebel even designed the paths to be wide enough for two children to walk along together. The children decided what they were going to plant and then had total responsibility for their plot (Tovey, 2008). Froebel used observations of children to develop his practice and believed in engaging the children in first-hand experiences to ensure they had a deep understanding of the concepts they were developing.

Margaret McMillan (1860–1931) developed her educational perspective through creating an outdoor camp for children in the slums of London. Disease was rife in the area and McMillan promoted the concept of outdoor play to improve the health of the children. The nursery was in fact the garden, and while there were some buildings, they were simply used as shelters in bad weather. McMillan believed in Froebel's theories, but while claiming not to be a follower of Montessori, she did believe in a more structured approach to learning than Froebel. McMillan did not create resources – she used what was natural; flowers and plants were chosen because of their different sensory properties and adults were encouraged to use these in questioning the children to help them learn. The whole garden was designed so that everything in it had a learning opportunity; steps were for jumping on and off, trees were for climbing. She also incorporated a heap of rubbish which encouraged the children to use their imagination and create whatever they wanted using found materials.

Maria Montessori (1869–1952) believed that it was scientific knowledge that underpinned a child's development. She created a 'Casa de Bambini' or children's house in Rome and everything within this was child sized, to enable children to take control of their environment. She too had a strong belief in the need for outdoor play and she promoted free access between the house and garden. Montessori had a very practical view of education; she did not see the need to develop a child's imagination or encourage play. The resources she provided had to be used in a certain way that she had planned and the plots in the garden were for growing vegetables that would be used for meals. While children were encouraged to engage in activities, they were structured and focused on developing a 'normalised child' (Montessori, 1949, p162) who behaved in an expected way, rather than developing an imaginative, creative child as Froebel and McMillan strived to do.

Susan Isaacs (1885–1948) Isaacs' theories were formulated from a totally different perspective from McMillan and Montessori. She worked with children from very privileged families and designed an experimental school which looked to encourage investigation and curiosity, and teach them about whatever they were most interested in. She encouraged children to take risks but also to take responsibility for their actions. They were allowed matches to make fires, but there were rules they had to follow, such as not building a fire next to the wooden summerhouse (Tovey, 2008). Isaacs used extensive observations on the children to extend her understanding of their development and needs.

Jean Piaget (1896–1980) Piaget was a psychologist who investigated the way children developed and learnt. He established that they went through a series of developmental stages (see Figure 11.1).

STAGES	AGE	CHARACTERISTICS
Sensori motor	0–2 years	Realises that objects are separate from themselves. Understands that they can cause something to happen, moving toys, banging to make sounds, etc. Understands that objects continue to exist even when out of sight.
Pre-operational	3–7 years	Is able to use language and to use pictures and words to name and illustrate objects. Is egocentric, does not understand that others may have different views. Only groups items by one feature, e.g. colour or shape.
Concrete operational	8–11 years	Uses a logical approach to understand objects and events. Can group items by identifying several common features and can use a single feature to order them.
Formal operational	11 years and above	Uses logic to understand abstract concepts and questions thinking. Is interested in theoretical ideas, such as the future.

Figure 11.1 Piaget's developmental stages. (Piaget, 2001)

Piaget also discussed his theories of learning through adaptation. He argued that initially children assimilate knowledge; that is, they see a new object and try to use it in the way they use similar objects. However, if this does not work they change their behaviour so that they can use it, and this is called accommodation. An example of this may be that a child has a bicycle and understands that something with wheels is called a bicycle and then the child sees a car; they assimilate this and call it a bicycle. The adult will tell the child that it is not a bicycle, that it is a car, the child then accommodates this idea and realises that not everything with wheels is a bicycle and that some are cars.

Lev Vygotsky (1896–1934) Vygotsky took the approach that children were able to extend their understanding through interacting with a 'more knowledgeable other'; this could be a peer, family member or educator. The child is operating at a level of actual development; with the support of another they can operate at a higher level. This is known as 'The Zone of Proximal Development' and will enable them to eventually achieve the level of potential development (Figure 11.2).

Vygotsky theorised that children learn in a social, interactive way and that learning takes place in any environment, not just a classroom.

Jerome Bruner (1915–) has been influential in bringing the work of Vygotsky to the attention of Western educationalists. He built on the work of Piaget, but like Vygotsky, he disagreed with Piaget's views of children as egocentric learners and believed that adults and peers played a very significant role in developing children's learning.

Bruner's research on child development led him to propose that there are three modes of representation (ways in which information is understood and stored in the memory). These

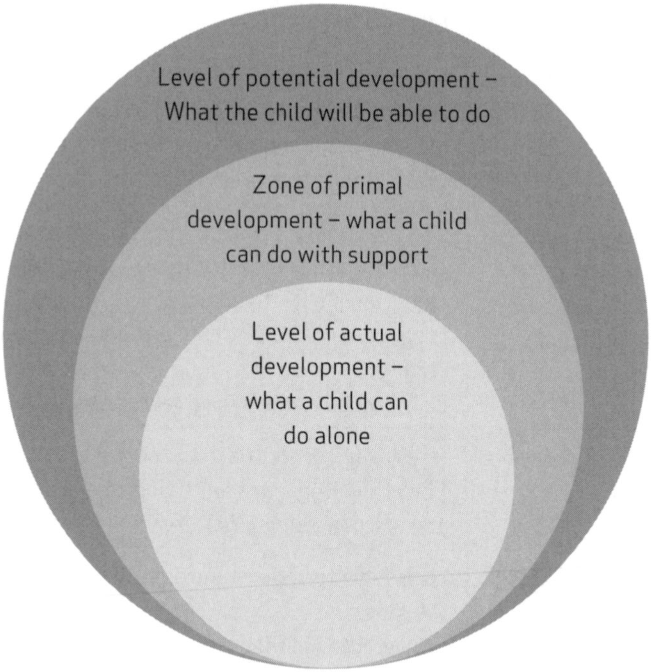

Figure 11.2 Vygotsky's Zone of Proximal Development. (Dolya, 2010)

modes of representation are fluid, each person develops at their own rate and when a child progresses to the next level, they do not stop using the previous one, but use whichever is suitable for the information they are engaging with (Figure 11.3):

Bruner suggested that children have the capacity to learn complex theories they are is presented in a way that is linked to their current understanding. He emphasised the importance of language in learning and, by using the appropriate level of language, concepts such as Archimedes' theory of displacement can be introduced to young children by drawing a line at the water level in the water tray, then adding heavy objects and letting the children see the change in the level. Little language is needed to introduce the idea, and vocabulary can be developed through discussion of the changes. Bruner valued play as an important tool for learning through doing.

Bruner also introduced the idea of the spiral curriculum. His research highlighted that what a child knows and understands is the starting point for any learning and that while teachers need to build on this and extend the child's understanding, previous learning needs to be revisited, linking existing ideas and concepts to new ones.

Tina Bruce: Bruce is a current, Frobelian theorist. She has been highly influential in developing early years education in Britain and has had leading roles in developing the Curriculum Guidance for the Foundation Stage, Birth to Three Matters and the Foundation Stage Profile.

Bruce emphasises that there are three defining factors in early years education. First, the child and who they are, what their experiences are and what their interests are at the current time; second, the context, the people around them, their emotional well-being, where they are and the resources they have access to; and third, the content, what is planned for them? What support will they receive? Is it relevant to their learning needs?

Enactive Representation (active engagement)	This is the most basic form of representation. Actions are remembered and stored in the memory. A baby remembers movements it makes that cause something to happen, for instance sucking and swallowing when it feeds, or moving its hand and knocking a rattle makes a noise.
Iconic Representation	At this stage, information is stored as images in the mind. Many people do this consciously, others do not realise they do this at all, though if you ask them what a dog looks like, they will be able to recall a visual image in order to describe it to you.
Symbolic Representation	This is the most sophisticated level of representation. Information is now stored as a symbol, such as language or a picture. This is a very flexible form of engaging with information, enabling the learner to manipulate it so that they can use imagination and developing knowledge and understanding to adapt previous concepts and consider new perspectives.

Figure 11.3 Bruner's modes of representation. (Smidt, 2011)

Bruce is a leading advocate of learning through play, and created ten principles of early years education.

1. The best way to prepare children for their adult life is to give them what they need as children.
2. Children are whole people who have feelings, ideas and relationships with others, and who need to be physically, mentally, morally and spiritually healthy.
3. Subjects such as mathematics and art cannot be separated; young children learn in an integrated way and not in neat, tidy compartments.
4. Children learn best when they are given appropriate responsibility, allowed to make errors, decisions and choices, and are respected as autonomous learners.
5. Self-discipline is emphasised. Indeed, this is the only kind of discipline worth having. Reward systems are very short-term and do not work in the long-term. Children need their efforts to be valued.
6. There are times when children are especially able to learn particular things.
7. What children can do (rather that what they cannot do) is the starting point of a child's education.
8. Imagination, creativity and all kinds of symbolic behaviour (reading, writing, drawing, dancing, music, mathematical numbers, algebra, role play and talking) develop and emerge when conditions are favourable.
9. Relationships with other people (both adults and children) are of central importance in a child's life.
10. Quality education is about three things: the child, the context in which learning takes place, and the knowledge and understanding which the child develops and learns.

(Bruce, 2005)

REFLECTIVE TASK

Familiarise yourself with the four underpinning principles of the Early Years Foundation Stage and link the theories we have examined to these principles. What connections can you make? Write a short reflective paragraph about how you have seen these theories and principles in practice and how you think understanding them could improve your practice.

Good communication and effective relationships

The most essential skills required by any practitioner working with any age group are communication skills. These will help you develop successful relationships with young children and their parents/carers. There is no doubt that the quality of children's lives depends on the quality of the relationships they themselves have with the people closest to them and the relationships between these people (Basquill et al., 2011). Research has shown that young children who have strong supporting relationships with the people closest to them develop into positive confident individuals, who can cope with separation and engage with others to learn and play (Bowlby, 1979; Doherty and Hughes, 2009). Government initiatives over the past decade have promoted the need for positive relationships, from the *Every Child Matters* Green Paper (DfES, 2003) to *Support for All: The families and relationships* Green Paper (DCSF, 2010) emphasising the understanding that having strong positive relationships promotes positive outcomes for children's health and well-being.

Being able to communicate effectively with young children requires using all your senses. They have limited or no language skills to draw upon. We all know that young babies cry when they need care and attention, and they soon learn how this works. The skill the adult requires is to work out what it is the baby needs. It may be your sense of smell is enough if it is nappy-changing time, but other needs require more sophisticated consideration. Many mothers have this ability tuned so finely that they instantly know a tired cry from a hungry cry, while an observer would be unable to tell the difference. Robinson (2008) explains how a good practitioner does not just use their ears to listen, but uses their eyes, heart and mind to pick up on the subtle, non-verbal communications used. Infant-directed speech (or motherese) is frequently used by adults to communicate with babies and young children. It involves using a higher pitch when speaking and is a natural response seen in many different cultures. It is effective because a baby's hearing is set at a higher level than an adult's so this way of speaking is clearer and more easily understood (de Boer, 2005). This can feel strange and uncomfortable to those not used to young children, but if understood as a recognised way of communicating by all practitioners, it can be quickly adopted and the positive effects will soon become apparent.

To ensure effective communication, the practitioner must ensure that they not only listen to what the child is communicating but that they value their thoughts, ideas and feelings and act upon them. All children have the right to be listened to and have their opinions respected and, if appropriate, acted upon (UNCRC, 1989).

All methods of communication used by young children need to be received positively. First attempts at mark making must be valued and can be used as a means of stimulating verbal communication. With this positive re-enforcement, the child will want to engage in this again and will develop enthusiasm for engaging in new activities.

Using these effective communication skills will develop a strong relationship between the child and the practitioner. Sylva et al. (2004) highlighted the importance of the quality of communication between children and practitioners, and that children made much better progress if there was a warm, responsive relationship between them.

It would not be possible for all practitioners to develop strong trusting relationships with every child in their setting and the EYFS strongly emphasises the need to actively engage with the Key Person process as this supports the principle of the Unique Child. Elfer et al. (2011) explain the benefits of this system, which enables one person to have the main responsibility for a small number of children. This enables them to develop a greater understanding of their likes and dislikes, individual needs and circumstances, and therefore allows them to support each child appropriately. This process is often backed up by having a second key person who will be able to take over when necessary to ensure stability and security for the children. This is not always a simple process, especially in a Reception class when staff to children ratios can be low, but it is still a benefit to the children if they understand that one particular adult is there to support them.

An essential aspect of developing the Key Person approach is developing trusting and constructive relationships with parents and carers. The EYFS highlights this as a significant part of the principle of Positive Relationships. It is important to realise the positive contributions parents/carers make to their children's education and to work with them to help them understand the way their children learn, and how they can support and extend that by engaging in activities at home. These relationships begin with the first contact with the setting. First impressions count and it is essential that parents/carers feel welcomed as soon as they show an interest in a place for their child. The practitioner needs to be welcoming, approachable, understanding and knowledgeable. The environment must also make them feel welcome and secure if you are expecting them to entrust their child to your care.

Once a good relationship has been established, it needs to be maintained, and the three-way relationship between child, parent/carer and staff must be respected. Having regular contact with parents, sharing their children's interests and working together to establish a cohesive approach to the care and education of the child ensures best outcomes for the child.

REFLECTIVE TASK

Think of your own experiences as a parent, or as a child, when walking into a school or nursery for the first time. Write down ten words that describe how you felt.

Now look at your own setting, walk through the door and really look around. What is the first thing you notice? How does it make you feel?

Think back to your list, does your setting address all of the issues you identified? Does it have the benefits you identified in your list?

Talk to some parents/carers that you have developed good relationships with, ask them to describe how they first felt when they entered the setting. Is there anything you could improve upon?

How do they feel now? What if anything has changed their opinion?

What action can you take to make the transition to your setting smoother for parents? Can you think of three strategies to engage parents more deeply with their child's learning?

Supporting young children's learning

Young children are often at the mercy of people and situations over which they have no control. Often these are minor and temporary problems but sometimes they can be major difficulties and the practitioner needs to identify these as soon as possible and be aware of the supportive procedures available to protect the child.

The first difficulty may well be the transition from home to the early years setting; this can be a massive change in a child's life. Moving from the security of the home environment to the independence, space and choices the setting offers can be a traumatic experience for many children. The Key Person approach again is essential to ease this. Home visits and accompanied visits to the setting lay the seeds of a bond that will blossom into a supportive and special relationship for the child. They will have a special person who they know they can come to when they feel insecure, who will give them the comfort and care they need to help them cope with all the new experiences they are going to have.

A common problem that affects a child's development and learning is the way transitions are managed. These are not limited to major transitions from home to nursery or nursery to reception, which may be the first that come to mind, or even the daily transition from the home to the setting, which can cause obvious difficulties such as separation anxiety. Many children can go through several transitions before they even arrive at the setting, with a variety of carers, who may be relatives or family friends involved; they may also spend time with child minders or in other settings. Fisher (2008) explains *Only when we see the world through a child's eyes do we truly understand just what is involved in making adjustments from one setting to the next.* All of these people will have different expectations, different relationships and different ways of managing behaviour. It is easy to see how difficult this could be for a young child to understand and cope with. Selleck (2006) highlights how these transitions happen to fit in with adult requirements and often the needs of the children are not regarded as important.

It is essential that early years practitioners are aware of the effects these transitions can have on a child. Their behaviour may change from day to day depending on how many transitions they have been through and the quality of them. The practitioners working with them need to be sensitive to this situation. They need to have good communication with parents and carers, emphasising the importance of some continuity for the child, even if that can only be the knowledge of who will pick them up at home time and where they will be going. That small amount of security can be sufficient to enable the child to relax and engage with provision. If the child goes to a childminder and/or another setting, family or friends, there needs to be some communication between everyone to ensure a consistent approach. Fisher (2008) suggests that all parties involved need to have a sound understanding of the effects of transition on a child, that all concerned should be involved in any decisions about the care of the child, that key people should have the opportunity to visit each other's provision to understand the similarities and differences, and all should share in observations assessments and planning. This supports the child in their understanding of what is expected of them, reduces confusion and consequently improves behaviour and engagement with learning.

Transferring from the early years setting to primary school is another major transition and again good communication between all parties is the key to making this an effective and positive experience for all. Working with parents to give advice if requested in making the right choice of school for the child may be the first step in this. It may also be necessary to support them if their child does not get a place in the school of choice, you may need to emphasise the positive aspects and help them work through any negative feelings they have.

Having strong relationships with local schools is of paramount importance; this will enable good communication, discussion of individual issues, opportunities for children to visit their new school and for members of staff to visit the children in the setting. Working collaboratively will create a strong supportive network of adults who will support every child, addressing their unique needs and ensuring that potentially stressful situations are avoided, and that the child feels safe, secure and confident enough to face these challenges with enthusiasm.

REFLECTIVE TASK
- Are you familiar with the Transition Policy in your setting?
- Does it cover all aspects of transition?
- How do you initiate and maintain relationships with other schools/settings?
- Do you involve colleagues from these settings in discussions about children you both care for?
- Select a child in your setting whose behaviour you are a little concerned about; talk to parents/carers and track the transitions this child goes through in a day. Are there any issues regarding transitions; how can you address these?

Welfare requirements

Ofsted will base its regulatory and inspection judgements on whether a provider has met the general and specific legal requirements, and has had regard to the statutory guidance.
(DCSF, 2008, p20)

One of the major changes brought about by the EYFS was the merging of education and care requirements of babies and young children. Previously, these had been separate issues and certain types of private, voluntary and independent settings would only engage in the care of children and, while the children naturally learnt through play activities, education was not a priority. Nursery classes and schools, on the other hand, were expected to educate the children. The Statutory Framework for the EYFS sets out the legal requirements for learning and development and for the welfare of babies and young children in all settings involved in their care.

The Order, the Regulations and the Statutory Framework document make up the legal basis of the EYFS. The requirements in this document have statutory force by virtue of the Childcare Act 2006. This means that all settings are required by law to adhere to these requirements to ensure that babies and young children receive the best care and education possible.

As an early years practitioner, you need to have a sound understanding of the welfare requirements, ensure that policies and procedures in your setting comply with them, and ensure that all colleagues, students and parents are aware of them and have access to them.

The welfare requirements cover essential issues such as the following.

Safeguarding and promoting children's welfare – Providers must ensure that they have staff trained in safeguarding children; they must promote a healthy lifestyle, take necessary steps to prevent the spread of infection, and take appropriate action when they are ill. Behaviour must be managed effectively and in a manner appropriate for their stage of development and particular individual needs, utilising a consistent approach to support the child's understanding

Suitable people – this addresses issues regarding safe recruitment, quality of staff, behaviour. Providers must ensure that adults looking after children, or having unsupervised access to them, are suitable to do so and have Criminal Record Bureau clearance. Adults looking after children must have appropriate qualifications, training, skills and knowledge. Staffing arrangements must be organised to ensure safety and to meet the needs of the children.

Suitable premises, environment and equipment – This addresses issues regarding risk assessment, premises and resources.

Organisation – this addresses issues regarding Key Person approach, equality of opportunity and ensuring a balanced curriculum.

Documentation – This addresses issues regarding records and data protection.

REFLECTIVE TASK
- Read the Statutory Framework for the EYFS. Do you have experience of addressing all the issues covered in the document?
- Does your setting have up-to-date policies in place addressing all these issues?
- Are there any areas you feel need developing? If so, how can you contribute to this to ensure the best provision and care for the children in your setting?

CHAPTER SUMMARY

In this chapter you learned:

- that good quality early years provision in education and care is essential to maximise child development and learning;
- that the Early Years Foundation Stage was produced to guide and direct practitioners working with young children so that they might maximise that learning and development in children;
- about the key theories and figures in early years practice and learning;
- that holistic care and education of the child is vital, with a multi-agency approach as central to that process.

REFERENCES

Allen, G. (2011) *Early Intervention: Next Steps*. London: HMSO.

Basquill, J., Beattie, L. and Ryan, J. (2011) *The EYPS Handbook*. London: Pearson.

Bowlby, J. (1979) *The Making and Breaking of Affectionate Bonds*. London: Tavistock.

Bruce, T. (2005) *Early Childhood Education*. London: Hodder Education.

de Boer, B. (2005) Infant directed speech and the evolution of language, in Tallerman, M. (ed.) *Evolutionary Prerequisites for Language*. Oxford: Oxford University Press, pp100–21.

Department for Children, Families and Schools (DCFS) (2008) *Statutory Framework for the Early Years Foundation*. Ref. 00267-2008-BKT-EN.pdf. London: DCSF.

Department for Children, Families and Schools (DCFS) (2010) *Support for All: The families and relationships*, Green Paper. London: DCSF.

Department of Education and Skills (DfES) (2003) *Every Child Matters*. Nottingham: DfES.

Doherty, J. and Hughes, M. (2009) *Child Development: Right from the start*. London: Pearson.

Dolya, G. (2010). *Vygotsky in Action in the Early Years: The key to learning curriculum*. London: Routledge.

Early Years Foundation Stage (EYFS) (2008) Available at www.education.gov.uk/publications/standard/publicationDetail/Page1/DCSF-00261–2008.

Elfer, P., Goldsschmeid, E. and Selleck, D. (2011) *Key Persons in the Nursery*. London: Routledge.

Fields, F. (2010) *The Foundation Years: Preventing poor children from becoming poor adults*. London: HMSO.

Fisher, J. (2008) *Starting from the Child*. Berkshire: Open University Press.

Gianoutsos, J. (2006) Locke and Rousseau: early childhood education. Baylor: *The Pulse*, 4(1).

Her Majesty's Government (HMG) (2010) *Support for All*. Norwich: TSO.

Mcmillan, M. (1919) *The Nursery School*. London: Dent.

Montessori, M. (1949) *The Absorbent Mind*. Madras: Kalakshetra Publications.

Piaget, J 2001, *Psychology of Intelligence*. Routledge eBook Collection (EBSCOhost), EBSCOhost, viewed 2/3/12.

Robinson, M. (2008) Child development: your guide to the first five years, Part 8. *Nursery World*, June.

Selleck, D. (2006) Key persons in the early years foundation stage, *Early Education* (Autumn).

Smidt, S. (2011) *Introducing Bruner: A guide for practitioners and students in early years education*. London: Routledge.

Sylva, K., Melhuish, E., Sammons, P., Siraj-Blatchford, I. and Taggart, B. (2004) *Effective Provision of Pre-School Education*. Nottingham: DfES.

Tickell, C. (2011) *The Early Years: Foundations for life, health and learning*. London: HMSO.

Tovey, H. (2008) *Playing Outdoors: Spaces and places, risks and challenge (debating play)*. Berkshire: Open University Press.

United Nations Convention on the Rights of the Child (1989) Geneva: Office of the High Commissioner for Human Rights.

12 EDUCATION IN THE TWENTY-FIRST CENTURY

Gillian Goddard and Anita Walton

CHAPTER OBJECTIVES

By the end of this chapter you will:

- have reflected on the present education system as part of a developing and changing provision;
- understand the various purposes of education;
- be able to speculate about future trends and developments, including those in support staff roles;
- understand some of the key influences on education development.

LINKS TO **HLTA** STANDARDS

1. Improve their own knowledge and practice.
2. Understand the key factors that affect children's and young people's learning and progress.

Introduction

Being involved in the daily practice of education delivery, it is sometimes hard to consider that the whole nature and provision of education could change. It is not that education delivery remains unchanging year on year; you will already be familiar with continuous small-scale change with wave after wave of government-led initiatives implemented in the last few years with an almost obsessive focus on improving standards of achievement. Many of you will be at the forefront of implementing those strategies and programmes, such as the intervention programmes for literacy and numeracy. Yet, in this chapter, I want you to step back and consider what is done in schools and why, in the light of your own educational experience as a child. I then want you to use your imagination to break free of the present structures and ways of doing things in education to reach into the future and speculate about the shape of schooling 20 years on.

To do this, we will need to explore what the whole point of education is and what influences its provision and objectives. In the latter half of the chapter we will focus particularly on new technologies and their impact on the world of teaching and learning. It is in this area that we have seen the greatest changes of practice.

What is education for?

There may well have been times when you have actually asked yourself the question, 'What is the point of this?' Aldrich, a social historian, wrote, rather tongue in cheek:

The term education might be applied to the process whereby society, or state, seeks to furnish itself with wise rulers, brave warriors, holy clerics, efficient businessmen, industrious workers and domesticated womenfolk.

(1982, p35)

REFLECTIVE TASK

Think for a moment about what Aldrich (1982) is saying here. Education has always been used, whether free or paid for, to create and maintain a stable, efficient, functioning and profitable society based on the development of vocational knowledge and skills. In Aldrich's (1982) view, it also involved, and still involves, the implicit indoctrination of an individual into their vocational 'place' in that society. Do you agree with that?

PRACTICAL TASK

Write down some notes on the way your educational setting actively develops future workplace skills and knowledge. What does it do that doesn't specifically enhance the pupils' chances of getting good jobs?

For example, teaching ICT skills is likely to have a direct relevance for employment requirements, but you might consider that teaching about the Tudors in history is not directly valuable for employability.

The purposes of education

There have been other important reasons why individuals and interest groups such as employers, the Church and the state have paid for their children to be taught something.

REFLECTIVE TASK

Try to think of as many reasons as you can for educating children and write them down.

Here are some reasons taken from the last two millennia.

Survival in life

This is the most fundamental and powerful reason for teaching children. Virtually all parents and families do this and are concerned with maximising their children's chances of keeping safe. Think about what you were taught by your family that helped you to keep safe.

Socialisation

We are social beings. We are programmed to live in groups and to survive better by co-operating with one another. The length of our maturation from infant to adulthood means that we are dependent on having one or more parents or carers living with us and tending to our needs. For this biological reason we need to be taught as children how to get on with people, how to compromise, how to lead, how to follow and how to read others' emotions and motives. Think again of how your family helped you to manage social relationships well.

Preparation for the workplace

Survival, and certainly 'getting on' in life, is largely dependent on the type of work we get. Much energy is spent and has always been spent in making children 'fit' for specific types of work. The apprenticeships of the medieval period, recently revived, were a formal expression of the need for the young (and not so young) to be given the opportunity to learn new skills associated with a particular job. You are doing that now, studying and developing your skills in the workplace.

Preservation of cultural values and identity

This has always been taught to children, whether in the family or community, or peer group or school. It is hard to define what is being taught, for values are often not explicitly taught but implicitly inculcated by dominant individuals and groups, where belonging depends on your adherence to a particular set of codes or beliefs. Indeed, your personal identity is often characterised by a set of communally held and transmitted values, given to you as children, then later acquired as part of your work. To consider what values and attitudes we encourage in school as part of our attempts at acculturation, have a look at the National Curriculum's *Statement of Values* (DfEE/QCA, 1999, pp147–9) and the most recent Teacher Standards which identify specific values to model and teach (DfE 2011a). Failing to successfully inculcate shared values creates difficulties for any society. Have you met any children whose family and community values and attitudes may be at odds with your own? I remember teaching Year 6 pupils in my first teaching practice when I was training to be a teacher. The school was in one of the most deprived areas of Liverpool. I urged the pupils to work hard at their maths and English so that they could get good jobs when they grew up. Most looked puzzled. Some were scornful. 'We won't get work', one chirped up, and it was a certainty in his mind. It was my first encounter with an alternative culture.

Improving potential earning power

Much of further and higher education is focused on achieving this purpose. It involves learning to earn more, to achieve personal wealth, power and status. Much of education at secondary school is also geared towards directing children into careers that not only match their aptitudes and talents, but also make them the most money and raise their status.

PRACTICAL TASK

Ask yourself what jobs carry high status in our society. What sort of jobs impress people? Now ask children you know what are the best jobs. They'll probably identify jobs that have a high income with, almost certainly, fame or celebrity attached. Successive governments have always prioritised education and training as part of this acknowledged drive to raise the personal wealth of society's members (DfE, 2010).

Self-realisation, or the realisation of innate potential

Ironically, this purpose only emerged in the early Victorian period when Dr Thomas Arnold, who became head of Rugby school, put forward the view that education was for something higher than wealth production and work skills. It was for character building, civilising, producing true Christians and turning boys into gentlemen (a reference to manners, not status) (Arnold, 2008). These ideas may seem archaic, but beneath this he felt that schools should help pupils to become the best people they can be. As an idea it appealed greatly in the post-war years after 1918, at least in the minds and hearts of most educators. Today, most of those involved in education directly aspire to this purpose.

PRACTICAL TASK

Spend time now thinking about what purposes our present system of state education would prioritise. Using the table, list those on which our system concentrates and put them in order of most important to least important. Now do this for yourself as an educator. An example has been included.

Education system priorities	My priorities
Work skills	Enjoyment of learning new knowledge and skills

Are your priorities, or the order of them, different from the 'official' ones? If so, what difference does that make to your pupils, yourself and the effectiveness of the organisation?

If you would like to read more about this potential conflict of purposes, I recommend reading Wilkins' article 'Is schooling a technology, a process of socialisation, or a consumer product?' in *Management in Education* (2005).

Influences on changes in education provision

We have always taught our children, albeit at home, in the community and at work. The ability and desire of the state to pay for the formal education of children, however, is more subject to fluctuating circumstances and the forces of change. There have been three main groups of forces that have led to change in formal education type and provision. The first group consists of philosophers and educationalists, and to these we can, today, add scientists and psychologists. They reform from within the education system by fundamentally objecting to the existing way of educating, then trying new things and promoting them as better ways. In the past their influence came in convincing practitioners that their system or way of educating was better than conventional practice. Some changes are short-lived, such as the ETA phonics spelling system tried in the 1960s; others are long term, such as the introduction of comprehensive education or co-educational schools (mixed boys and girls).

Currently, concerns from educationalists about the very nature of primary education, in all its aspects, has led to the independent primary education review led by Rob Alexander at

Cambridge University (Alexander, 2009). Its interim reports have severely criticised the structure, practices and priorities of the present system and its final report was revolutionary in its conception of primary schooling and the curriculum (Alexander, 2009). In response, the former government set up its own primary review led by Jim Rose (DCSF, 2008c) to counteract the impact of such criticism, though, this new Rose curriculum was killed at birth by the succeeding coalition government in 2010 when it came to power. Interestingly, the new Government has launched its own review of the curriculum and proposed a radical shake-up of state education (DfE, 2010). Guy Claxton (2008) has also just recently published his own critique of the English education system. You might be interested in reading more about what these critics say and judge for yourselves the merits of their cases. Their publication details can be found at the end of this chapter.

The second group of forces centres around those who hold sufficient power to enforce change. Formerly, this would have been kings and queens and the Church, but nowadays this is seen most clearly in central government policy and funding, or lack of it. This is the most obvious driver for change that we currently experience. Consider the new initiatives you are aware of that have been introduced in the last ten years. Some are mandatory and universally undertaken, such as Every Child Matters, the 14–19 curriculum, the Early Years Foundation Stage, performance management, remodelling the workforce and synthetic phonics. Others are initiatives that tend to be funded only in the short term, but are often universal in their coverage, such as the intervention literacy and numeracy catch-up programmes, 'Lads and Dads' literacy programmes to raise boys' underachievement or learning mentors, although, in this case, schools now self-fund these as they are so effective.

The third group of forces comes from outside the education system. It can best be described as 'outside forces', such as war, economic depression (highly relevant in this current decade), deep poverty, times of plenty, political doctrine or ideology such as totalitarian states or those influenced by strict application of religious law, and, of great significance for the whole world, the growth of technologies. This last factor will be addressed later, but the others all impact powerfully on education provision and its nature. When we entered the Second World War, children were evacuated from cities, causing overpopulation in rural schools and the initial closure of city schools. Teachers had been enlisted into the armed forces, leaving fewer available nationally. Later, when the children returned to cities, we experienced the Blitz, which decimated school buildings and led to schools running a morning and afternoon school session, with pupils attending either in the morning or afternoon. The schools concentrated on core subjects and PE. There were virtually no resources and no money for repairs and facilities. Classes were large and children were traumatised and exhausted. Contrast that with our provision today and the environment and facilities we have access to. In poorer countries education is a luxury, available only to those who can pay.

REFLECTIVE TASK
Spend a few minutes considering what are the most powerful outside forces affecting your role and setting.

The 'what' of education: past, present and future

One of the ways of anticipating future trends in education is to think about aspects of education provision separately. The curriculum we teach, that is the subjects and subject content, has not remained static. Think back to your own school days. What subjects were you taught in primary and secondary school? I was educated in the 1960s and early 1970s. In primary we had nature walks and French, as well as English, maths and RK (religious knowledge). We did do science but it was taught by listening to the schools radio programme. In my second primary school we only did maths and English in the morning, then the girls did needlework and played rounders, while the boys played football in the afternoons. At secondary school the girls did domestic science and the boys did woodwork and metalwork. There was no IT because it didn't exist.

Consider the curriculum today. We've had the application of a compulsory government-determined curriculum since 1988. Science has been elevated to a core subject alongside maths and English, and ICT is also very important. The place of modern foreign languages has been disputed and altered at both primary and secondary phases and it is still under review (DfE, 2010). Personal, social and health education (PSHE) and citizenship have also made an appearance and, although mostly non-mandatory, their place as a key element of the curriculum is currently being debated (Best, 1999; Crow 2008; DfE, 2010). The emergence of alternative curricula in Wales and Northern Ireland has added a comparative challenge to the dominance of the English National Curriculum (Aasen and Waters, 2006). We are seeing the growth of metacognition skills work being actively taught, e.g. how to think and solve problems (Claxton, 2002).

You may wish to look at the Steiner Waldorf Schools Fellowship school curriculum. It is very successful but radically different from our own National Curriculum (www.steinerwaldorf. org.uk).

> **PRACTICAL TASK**
> What will our curriculum in schools look like in 2020? Will it look like your independent school? Will it be very similar to our present one or will there be no 'national curriculum'? Will that have been abandoned in favour of local school, local authority, open schools, academies or parental choice? Discuss this with your peers. See if you can predict the future provision.

The how of education: past, present and future

Pedagogy or teaching methods have also been subject to considerable change, particularly with regard to the ideological battle between 'talk and chalk' instructional modes of teaching, promoted by the government-sponsored report by Alexander et al. (1992) re-enforced by the present Secretary of State for Education (DfE, 2011b), and 'facilitation' of learning through independent and pupil initiated activities, currently being reinvigorated as part of the Early Years Foundation Stage. Despite that, good practice has remained fairly constant, based on Galton et al.'s (1990) 'Fitness for Purpose' principle. This argues that teaching well requires the deployment of a mixture of teaching methods at appropriate times.

REFLECTIVE TASK

Think of the last lesson that you observed or in which you participated.

- When, if at all, did the teacher instruct, explain to and question the whole class? (Instructional mode)
- Did the teacher have the pupils undertake group or independent activities? (Facilitation)
- Was there a whole class plenary? (Re-enforcement)

Now think about your own practice.

- What teaching methods did you use?
- Did you explain the task, reword or demonstrate?
- Did you question and observe as tasks were undertaken?
- Did you stop the pupils and explain an issue with which many were having difficulty?
- Did you choose the right methods to achieve the objectives or were you constrained by the environment or prevailing teaching approaches?
- How would you have taught that session ideally?

Future changes in teaching methods may rest with neuroscience and technological developments. It is in these two fields that we have seen the greatest change of approach, the former with the introduction of methods such as brain gym, VAK (visual, audio, kinaesthetic) learning styles, awareness and metacognition or learning power approaches (Dommett et al., 2011; Claxton, 2002). The latter has led to the use of more internet- and computer-based media, especially the interactive whiteboard, discussed below.

The former government also threw its weight behind pedagogy reforms such as personalised learning, while the coalition government favours traditional teaching methods, especially favouring the memorising and recitation of knowledge (DfE, 2011).

The where of education: past, present and future

Education doesn't have to take place in a building we would know as a school. Most of our education takes place at home and among our communities. Yet for at least a thousand years pupils have been brought together, initially in monasteries and churches, to be taught. Later, grammar schools were founded for boys. By the late nineteenth century there was a massive expansion of elementary schools to meet the requirements of the Education Act 1870, which made education universally available for all children, boys and girls, between the ages of 5 and 10. The making of universal and free secondary education in 1944 saw a similar expansion of secondary school buildings (Richards, 2006). It is from this legacy that we have our present school buildings, locally provided, reduced in grounds as a result of the playing field 'sell-off' of the 1990s and 2000s and with specialist facilities. Now the drive is towards privately supported academies and 'free-schools', so we are likely to see far more diversity in structure and form of schools in the future (DfE, 2011a; DfE, 2011b).

REFLECTIVE TASK

Consider the design of your school buildings. What types of room or space are provided? Why do we have those spaces? Think about the hall. Why do we have that big space? Think about other specialist spaces such as laboratories, or ICT suites, art areas or gymnasia. Does your school have a kitchen and a dining room or canteen? Why was that developed? Fifty years ago, pupils all went home for dinner. What about the classroom spaces? What shape are they? Why are they like that? What fitments are provided? Do you have your own specialist support base? What determines that shape? School buildings are remarkably similar. Consider whether that is because architects lack imagination or we use old buildings, or because those shapes and spaces are fit for purpose.

I want to conclude this discussion by considering the possible development of places of education, other than what we would recognise as schools. We have seen the emergence of academies of learning, which, for all the name change, we would recognise as schools, but there are moves to offer a range of alternative settings for learning, such as FE colleges, the workplace and centres such as football clubs, children's centres, home learning and web-based learning in small community cells, based on the models adopted in Finland and Australia, where children are scattered in remote areas.

The drive for alternative settings for education in Britain stems not from geographical difficulties, but social and motivational problems for pupils. More and more parents are educating their children at home because they simply don't feel their children would thrive emotionally or educationally at a school (Freedom for Children to Grow, 2007). Many of the alternative settings are being created as part of the *Every Child Matters Agenda*, for children who have become disaffected with the institution we call school. In fairness, this is not just about place, but also about the curriculum, the pace of learning and the social climate of the setting.

There has also been criticism about the large size of schools, especially in secondary settings. There has been successful piloting of big schools splitting up into small sub-schools that are self-contained and share the same staff and spaces, creating smaller, safer and more easily monitored school communities. This is aimed at tackling the pupils' sense of being lost, anonymous and unsafe, as reported in the Good Childhood survey (Children's Society, 2006).

If we consider the future of 2020, will we see more use of these alternative venues? Will we see big secondary and primary schools split up organisationally and geographically to support the psychological and safety needs of pupils? If not, what will stop that development? What is your view?

Perhaps it is in the field of technological innovation that the answer to our future education system lies.

E-learning

Education in the twenty-first century will almost certainly involve the exploitation of information and communication technology (ICT), and both teachers and Teaching Assistants

(TAs) will be required to acquire ICT capability for its effective integration into the classroom. We often hear the word 'e-learning' used and how it can create new learning environments. If someone is using ICT when learning, they are using e-learning. According to the DfES (2003):

> *E-learning exploits interactive technologies and communication systems to improve the learning experience. It has the potential to transform the way we teach and learn across the board. It can raise standards, and widen participation in lifelong learning. It cannot replace teachers and lecturers, but alongside existing methods it can enhance the quality and reach of their teaching, and reduce the time spent on administration. It can enable every learner to achieve his or her potential, and help to build an educational workforce empowered to change. It makes possible a truly ambitious education system for a future learning society.*

Here are some examples of e-learning:

- a child using an interactive game;
- a pupil using software that has been installed on school computers to complete activities;
- pupils in a geography lesson using computers to complete a virtual field trip.

Below are some examples of why schools are using e-learning.

- It makes teachers more efficient in preparation, assessment and recording.
- Teachers and TAs can use e-learning to personalise the learning experience for pupils.
- Pupils can access resources at home.
- Pupils can learn at their own pace.
- Lessons can be presented in an exciting way.
- Computer systems can mark work, giving immediate feedback.
- Pupils are not totally reliant on the teacher.
- E-learning can expand the community of learners beyond the classroom.

REFLECTIVE TASK

Think of more examples of e-learning that you have seen in school, and then for each example think of why it was used. Did it improve the learning experience?

ICT and literacy

Some teachers feel that the use of books is more likely to raise standards in English than ICT. Slater (2003), in an article in *The Times Educational Supplement*, accuses Ofsted of being more likely to be impressed by a school's ICT equipment than by its books. Schools spend three times more on ICT than on books, but it is not significant in raising standards. According to Slater, spending on books is more likely to improve pupils' academic performance. According to Johnson (2008), however, in an article in *The Guardian*, statistics that report that reading is on the decline completely fail to consider the amount of reading that we do every day on our computers.

Watson (2002), in his study of schoolbook spending in 1,500 schools, asked teachers to what extent they believed that book stocks are effective in raising standards. The results showed that

90 per cent of primary teachers and 87 per cent of secondary teachers in the study thought that book stocks were effective or highly effective in raising standards. When asked the same question about ICT provision, the results were lower, with 67 per cent of secondary teachers rating it as effective and 50 per cent of primary teachers. It seems that, while most teachers see book stocks as being more effective in raising standards than ICT provision, the majority of teachers feel that ICT also has a part to play in improving academic achievement in English.

Watts and Lloyd (2004), in their paper, 'The use of innovative ICT in the active pursuit of literacy', looked at whether 'Espresso for Schools' (which is a multimedia ICT package) promoted learning. Espresso delivers educational content every week that provides resources for pupils and teachers related to the National Curriculum. It provides television-quality sound and pictures, and the materials for pupils include activities, tasks and games. There is a teacher staffroom to support the materials.

According to Watts and Lloyd, Espresso produced high levels of motivation and helped in the teaching of journalistic writing styles. The pupils found Espresso to be a reliable source of knowledge and information, and the teacher was seen as facilitating learning, rather than being the expert provider of information. The learning experience was constructivist in that the teacher did not directly give instructions and there was much pupil autonomy as they developed their written work into a tabloid newspaper form. Graphics and text features helped pupils to present their news articles in a journalistic style. Constructivism is a theory of learning that sees the purpose of learning as a person's construction of his or her own meaning, which focuses on primary concepts, rather than memorising facts. Constructivism is a philosophy of learning founded on the premise that each of us selects our own 'mental models', which we use to make sense of our experiences. We construct new ideas based upon the knowledge we already have, to accommodate new experiences. The teacher should encourage pupils to learn through discovering ideas and knowledge for themselves. Rather than learning the definitions of concepts, they should understand the meaning of them (Novak, 1988).

The research mentions that the software encouraged collaboration, which was ascertained from interviews with teachers and pupils, and observations in the lessons. The key messages from Watts and Lloyd's research are that innovative software can enhance learning, but this may require a different approach to pedagogy with responsibility for learning being devolved from teacher to learner.

Another innovative use of ICT in the pursuit of understanding difficult literacy texts is an educational software known as Kar2ouche, which is a storyboard program designed by collaboration between software designers and professional educators as part of an initiative funded by Intel and based at Oxford University. Kar2ouche and its module 'Macbeth' were evaluated by Peter Birmingham from Oxford University and Chris Davies from 'Immersive Education', who produced the software (Birmingham and Davies, 2001). The purpose of the evaluation was to be formative in order to develop a prototype, and then research and develop an understanding of its organisational and cognitive aspects.

Kar2ouche has a storyboarding facility that enables pupils to select images and text from a play, which are all stored on a databank. Pupils can change the direction in which characters face and can change the setting of the scene. In addition, they can change the posture of a character to suggest anger, happiness, etc. The intention is that storyboarding can have an impact on their understanding of text and scenes in the play. Kar2ouche trials took place in three different English classes and the teachers were asked to look at ways in which they could use it to help them achieve their existing aims for studying Macbeth. Birmingham and Davies felt it was important that the teachers did not change their existing teaching and learning aims to accommodate the software, and they were asked to accommodate the software into their existing lesson plans.

Birmingham and Davies (2001) believe that the work the pupils were engaged in during the construction of the storyboards is embedded in the conversations that took place between the members of the group. Their research highlights how this software enabled pupils to understand complex language and concepts through interaction between teacher, students and software. The opportunity for collaborative work was not just about taking turns with the mouse and keyboard; instead, Kar2ouche was able to stimulate discussion, focusing on particular scenes and text.

PRACTICAL TASK
List in the table below examples of software used in your school and whether it is passive or whether it involves collaboration and interaction among pupils.

Software	Passive	Collaborative/Interactive
Kar2ouche		✓

Do you think that discourse is important when pupils learn?

Technology and the future

Schools in the future will continue to use e-learning, and technology in education will continue to be promoted as a way to transform learning. Sometimes, when using passive software, pupils remain unchallenged or the lessons can be highly skills oriented. Becker (2000) suggests that teachers should support constructivist pedagogies, rather than a transmission-oriented pedagogy, emphasising group work involving discourse, which goes beyond skills-oriented software. In addition, both Vygotskian and neo-Vygotskian approaches see learning occurring in a social context before becoming internalised, and classwork is achieved collaboratively through interaction among pupils. Discourse is particularly important, as it is the way pupils share experience, through which understandings are constructed (Wegerif and Scrimshaw, 1997).

CHAPTER SUMMARY

- Education appears static and unchanging, but in practice it has always been subject to change and quite fundamental changes at that.
- To understand the structure and nature of education provision, it is important to identify the purposes of education that are dominant at any one time. These include simple survival and the generation of personal and national wealth, global competition, vocational skills development and perpetuating and developing civilised society, as it is perceived by those in charge.
- Change in education provision is often influenced by thinkers and educationalists themselves, political paymasters and outside forces, such as technological and scientific developments, conflict, the state of the economy, nationally, regionally and globally, and political and religious ideologies.
- The future of education will be marked by possible changes in curricula and in teaching methods, including the government's focus on developing personalised learning and meeting the five outcomes of *Every Child Matters*, which it most recently outlined in its visionary document, *The Children's Plan: Building brighter futures* (DCSF, 2008a) and its education-specific follow-up document, *Promoting Excellence for All* (DCSF, 2008b).
- It is that all-encompassing demand for every child to be enabled to learn in a safe, happy and effective way that has led to the consideration of alternative settings other than schools for education.
- In the end, advancing technologies may have the greatest impact on education, in all aspects of delivery; however, the technologies used must remain servants to effective pedagogy and should enhance teaching and learning.
- The future is an exciting and challenging prospect.

REFERENCES

Aasen, W. and Waters, J. (2006) The new curriculum in Wales: a new view of the child?, *Education 3–13*, 34(2): 123–9.

Aldrich, R. (1982) *An Introduction to the History of Education*. London: Hodder & Stoughton.

Alexander R. (ed.) (2009) *Children, Their World, Their Education: Findings and recommendations of the Cambridge Primary Review*. London: Routledge.

Alexander, J., Rose, J. and Woodhead, C. (1992) *Curriculum Organisation and Classroom Practice in Primary Schools*. London: DES.

Arnold, T. (2008) *The Miscellaneous Works of Thomas Arnold*. Charleston: BiblioBazaar.

Becker, H.J. (2000) Findings from the Teaching, Learning, and Computing Survey: Is Larry Cuban right? Revision of a paper written for the School Technology Leadership Conference of the Council of Chief State School Officers, Washington, DC, January. Available online at www.crito.uci.edu/tlc/findings/ccsso.pdf (accessed 11/8/08).

Best, R. (1999) Pastoral care and the millennium, in Collins, U. and McNiff, J. (eds) *Rethinking Pastoral Care*. London: Routledge.

Birmingham, P. and Davies, C. (2001) Storyboarding Shakespeare: learners' interactions with storyboard software in the process of understanding difficult literacy texts. *Technology, Pedagogy and Education*, 10(3): 241–56, October.

Children's Society (2006) Good Childhood? A question for our times. Available online at www.childrenssociety.org.uk/what-we-do/research (accessed 3/3/12).

Claxton, G. (2002) *Building Learning Power: Helping young people to become better learners*. London: TLO.

Claxton, G. (2008) *What's the Point of School? Rediscovering the heart of education*. London: Oneworld.

Crow, F. (2008) Learning for well-being: personal, social and health education and the changing curriculum. *Pastoral Care in Education*, 26(1): 43–51.

Department for Children, Schools and Families (DCSF) (2008) *Independent Review of the Primary Curriculum*. Available online at www.education.gov.uk/publications/eOrderingDownload/IPRC_Report.pdf (accessed 2/3/12).

Department for Education (2010) The Schools White Paper: *The Importance of Teaching*, London: DfE.

Department for Education (2011a) *About Academies*. Available online at www.education.gov.uk/schools/leadership/typesofschools/academies (accessed 30/9/11).

Department for Education (2011b) Free Schools Conference. Available online at www.education.gov.uk/schools/leadership/typesofschools/freeschools (accessed 30/9/11).

Department for Education and Employment/Qualifications and Curriculum Authority (DfEE/QCA) (1999) The National Curriculum, key stages 1 and 2. London: HMSO.

Department for Education and Skills (DfES) (2003) *The Skills for Life Survery: A national needs and impact survey of literacy, numeracy and ICT skills*. London: HMSO.

Dommett, E., Devonshire, I. and Chruches, R. (2011) *Learning and the Brain Pocketbook*, Winchester: Teachers Pocket Books.

Freedom for Children to Grow (2007) *The Home Education Campaign*. Available online at http://freedom.edyourself.org/headlines.htm (accessed 2/3/12).

Galton, M., Simon, B. and Croll, P. (1990) *Inside the Primary Classroom*. London: Routledge.

Johnson, S. (2008) *Dawn of the Digital Natives: Is reading declining?* Available online at www.guardian.co.uk/technology/2008/feb/07/internet.literacy (accessed 11/8/08).

Novak, J. (1998) *Learning, Creating and Using Knowledge*. Mahwah, NJ: Lawrence Erlbaum Associates.

Richards, C. (2006) The establishment of English primary education 1941–1946, *Pastoral Care in Education*, 34(1): 5–10.

Slater, J. (2003) Books lose their appeal, *Times Educational Supplement*, 26 September.

Watson, R. (2002) *Schoolbook Spending in the UK 2001/2002*. London: Educational Publishers Council.

Watts, M. and Lloyd, C. (2004) The use of innovative ICT in the active pursuit of literacy, *Journal of Computer Assisted Learning*, 20: 50–8.

Wegerif, R. and Scrimshaw, P. (1997) *Computer and Talk in the Primary Classroom*. Clevedon: Multilingual Matters.

Wilkins, R. (2005) Is schooling a technology, a process of socialisation, or a consumer product?, *Management in Education*, 19(1): 25–31.

Further reading

Dent, H.C. (1982) *Education in England and Wales*. London: Hodder and Stoughton.

Holmes-Beck, R. (1965) *A Social History of Education*. New York: Prentice Hall.

Newby, M. (2005) *A Learner's Curriculum: Towards a curriculum for the twenty-first century*. London: ATL.

Library & IT Centre
Trafford College
Manchester Road
West Timperley
Altrincham
Cheshire
WA14 5PQ

Index